SAVAGE ON SELLING
Secrets from an Insurance Great

JOHN SAVAGE, CLU

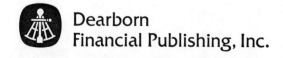

Dearborn
Financial Publishing, Inc.

While a great deal of care has been taken to provide accurate and current information, the ideas, suggestions, general principles and conclusions presented in this text are subject to local, state and federal laws and regulations, court cases and any revisions of same. The reader is thus urged to consult legal counsel regarding any points of law—this publication should not be used as a substitute for competent legal advice.

Publisher: Kathleen A. Welton
Acquisitions Editor: Patrick J. Hogan
Associate Editor: Karen A. Christensen
Senior Project Editor: Jack L. Kiburz
Interior Design: Lucy Jenkins
Cover Design: The Charles Marketing Group, Ltd.

Printed in the United States of America

94 95 96 10 9 8 7 6 5 4 3 2 1

Library of Congress Cataloging-in-Publication Data

Savage, John, 1930–1993
    Savage on selling : secrets from an insurance agent / by John
Savage.
        p. cm.
    Includes index.
    ISBN 0-7931-0913-2
    1. Insurance, Life—Agents. 2. Selling. I. Title.
HG8876.S259 1994   93-46054
    368.3'2'00688—dc20   CIP

Contents

Acknowledgments

I would like to thank David M. Drury, who spent many hours with me in the writing and development of this book. I am also indebted to the following librarians for their generous assistance in helping locate the many sources of statistical data cited in this book as well as background information relating to various business and government trends: Colleen Palmer and Bess Wood (Government Documents and Business departments, respectively), The Jerome Libraries, Bowling Green State University; Campbell Brady, The Toledo-Lucas County Public Libraries.

Foreword: A Son's Remembrance . . .

On February 8, 1993, John F. Savage died at age 62, following a 40-day battle with acute leukemia. He finished this book two months prior to his death. It represents the final chapter in his legacy as a great humanitarian and sales giant.

John Savage did not write a page of his four books for himself; he was anything but self-serving. He would have been far happier watching ESPN, drinking grape juice and spending time with wife, Kate, and family than composing.

This work is the result of his wanting to pass on the knowledge and methods that made him a success in all aspects of his life. From the spiritual to the intellectual, from the family unit to the office unit, he was a winner. In essence, his wish for anyone reading this book was that they reap the happiness and benefits that accompanied his 42 years in the insurance industry. Many had the pleasure of listening to him talk formally, as well as on less formal occasions—say, in the corner of some hotel lobby at midnight. I sympathize with those who never had the good fortune to meet him. They missed the opportunity to revel in the company of a unique man.

As his son of 19 years, I observed the most special individual I have ever encountered, excluding my mother. His death leaves a void in my life that will never be filled. I feel blessed for the times we spent together; we had a relationship, as did the rest of his children, that could otherwise be made possible only by way of a fairy tale.

He always said his job as a father was to love, not to be loved. I could not love anyone more; that is what lives on in me.

Here are his sales ideas, one-liners and prescription for making it in the industry . . . and in life. I can only hope you will hear his message and apply it to your best advantage. I believe your rewards for doing so will be substantial. There would be nothing he'd wish for more than having you adapt his practices to your personal touch: The High Touch.

—Aaron Savage
March 1993

Preface

Savage on Selling is my fourth book on the subject of sales. Why another? Because in the past several years I've added to what has proven to be one of the most productive sales techniques in the insurance industry—and I want to pass along these new approaches and modifications. Also, after intense analysis of the treatment of the selling profession in higher education and in corporate America, I want to address this problem, which I consider to be of paramount importance not only to the insurance industry but also to the entire sales arena, whatever the product.

My overall perception of selling in the United States is analogous to beholding the classic portrait of Dorian Gray: handsome on the outside but, when you look at the real picture, extraordinarily ugly within. It bears all the symptoms of eventual decay, along with self-inflicted wounds capable of drastically curtailing commerce of every stripe, and threatens to further degenerate a society already overburdened with afflictions. In a nutshell, there's an awful lot of correcting to do to right the wrongs of a troubled sales occupation. Otherwise, in my opinion, we're courting an unprecedented societal disaster. That isn't hyperbole for the sake of attention-getting; collectively, we're all in the same quicksand.

On the corporate side—where my conclusions were drawn from close-ups of businesses with between 2,000 and 3,000 employees—sales negatives are so deep and pervasive that it's almost unimaginably depressing. Specifically, there is a corporate myopia when it comes to what I contend is the fundamental selling process. True, some salespeople are making a lot of money; but many do so at the expense of their colleagues. As a rule, the latter are trapped in a management-ordained procedure that equalizes sales force income despite unequal individual productivity. The real effect is a slap at the high achievers, with no genuine improvement among the sales mediocrities and laggards.

Rather than promote what I contend are the basic essentials of building relationships/clientele to better serve society (with a multiplicity of rewards to follow!), the system has produced an epidemic of those who, on a 10-point scale, rate making money as numbers 1 through 10. No one so inclined has ever come close to persuading me that this is the enlightened view. Too frequently, that pattern causes breakdown in other areas I deem extremely important. While those people have lots of toys, they also have a chaotic family life, are devoid of spiritual anchorage and the morality that flows from it, and wind up their lives with a dollar sign for an epitaph.

The roots of the corporate dilemma are many. Among the peskiest is sales force "standardization." It's "Hey, gang, we're all part of a 'team'!" Translation: Don't rock the boat; exhibit concern for strengthening the weak (salesman); don't jeopardize morale by selling twice as much as the other guy. Spread the loot without regard to an individual's productivity. Because I love athletics so much, let me draw a sports parallel: Humongous Corporation runs the Chicago Bulls. At one of innumerable meetings, the CEO looks somewhat sadly but resignedly at his most prolific player and pontificates, "Michael, your shooting is hurting the team's morale. You've simply got to bring your points down to 17–18 per game!" With that kind of leadership, the Bulls would be anything but winners. Yet, nutty as it may sound, that's the sort of rationale that guides corporate selling.

Working together is a concept that has a place in a sales organization. But is *must* afford full accommodation for the salesperson who excels. Equality is a beautiful principle as espoused by the Declaration of Independence. But we all know from personal experience, as well as from biblical references, that all men are not created equal. For those to whom much is given, much is expected. Our gifts are distributed unevenly. It may not be "fair," but it sure is reality.

Let me put forth this contention: Financially reward a sales leader (with better than average skills) according to his or her proven productivity and you'll not only be "fair" to that person, you'll also very likely DOUBLE the sales performance of the guy or gal at the bottom of the ladder. Contrary to what some may believe, the also-rans won't just throw in the towel and give up because a few top producers reap their just rewards—not if their sales management is on the ball! If it is, those on the lower rungs will be given a substantial incentive to double their output. And I firmly believe that outcome is totally realistic!

Cynics may say that I'm espousing a tactic that would promote the philosophy of doing anything to make a sale. Well, I certainly wouldn't condone such an attitude—nor would any sales manager worth his or her salt. It would completely contradict the dictum of building *lasting* relationships with *satisfied* clientele whom you seek to *serve.* You cannot do that by pressing for a signature, then bolting for the door. As a good old friend, Woody Woodson, put it, "It's not the gale but the set of the sail that makes the ship move."

I'm going to expand on integrity, respect for the client, the concern to serve (and not to be served) and elimination of negatives. But I'm not writing here strictly for salespeople. I also want this book to open a window and perhaps admit some fresh air and understanding of what's happening in sales generally—and the consequences. Further, I want the message to reach our citadels of learning so that they'll recognize the pressing need for a solid, comprehensive course load leading to a degree in sales. Sales classes generally offered now run from poor to pathetic. I will lay before you just how poorly our colleges and universities serve the needs of one of the most important elements in our economy as well as in our society.

With the proper attention paid to selecting and training young people for careers in sales, we'll hear less wailing about jobs drying up. Sure, I'm after a monumental change, starting at the corporate *and* educational levels. In relative terms, we're still in the embryonic stage. (Perhaps it would move the process along if we could display a "typical" corporate sales meeting on national TV—with its predictable ratings debacle.) But what a huge difference it could make in, say, the next 20 years: bright kids, highly motivated, well prepared and continually trained, grabbed up by receptive, eager, productivity-oriented employers. Big companies learning from the small, entrepreneur-driven firms that are headed by the best salespeople in the world—and who can form the launching pad for universities to reorganize their curricula to produce generations of outstanding sellers.

The potential spinoffs of getting our national sales act together are as limitless as they are mind-boggling: a continuous doubling of sales—not just for the bucks, but for far, far more. Success in selling can be highly infectious, permeating every nook and cranny of the benefited organization: better sales; better product development; more jobs; the wherewithal to mitigate the horrors of unemployment and the crime, substance abuse and broken homes that come in its wake; more disposable income for better schools and medical services; and on and on. In short, I'm forging a definite link between the potential for improvement of selling and the potential for a much-improved society. Farfetched? Maybe. But read on and judge for yourself whether *Savage on Selling* knows whereof it speaks.

PART ONE

The Savage
"High Touch"

1

The Basics:
Face to Face

We'll begin with some overview observations, a few fundamentals and some pertinent principles. Later, we'll get into a thorough rundown of specific examples and their applications.

All this comes to you from one who has had the good fortune of devoting most of his life to selling and of enjoying beyond words a beautiful wife and family. I couldn't dream of asking for more than I've long since received.

That's not to say it all just fell into place, or that I was the so-called natural. In fact, I spent at least the first ten years of my career maturing and groping. I was looking for the formula that would enable me to perform for the betterment of all whom I served. I also sought to help salespeople avoid the many obstacles I encountered—problems, misinformation and disillusion—that are clearly avoidable. From roughly 40 years of professional hindsight, I worked out a personal niche that I identify as my servant/leadership role. As I've been highly motivated to serve my clients beyond their expectations, I've been similarly driven to lead in terms of salesperson development. Toward the latter, I offer a lifetime of singularly successful salesmanship, as well as the belief that I owed the profession for substantially more than merely collecting an unbroken string of paychecks.

Put another way, I hope to help those in sales who are inundated with information that, however well-meaning, will not help them to be effective. Ironically, I suspect that most of our leaders are salespeople. But they don't realize what the most important things are that will bring about their effectiveness. For example, the big corporate buzzword currently is "empowerment." It's a term I've tried to apply to everyone working with me throughout my entire life. It reflects a thoughtful, dynamic philosophy. On the other hand, I'm convinced that, via empowerment or its like, a great many people are doing things very, very well that they shouldn't even be doing.

THE PROOF IS IN THE PROCESS

In my lectures, I occasionally note that dogs instinctively turn aside when they see a ditch too deep and wide. Not human beings; they plunge in, one right after the other. Far too often, bad information is taught (unwittingly) and blindly accepted. Both teacher and student mean well, but good intentions on either side do not overcome a defective process.

Plato admonished, "Know thyself." I don't know for sure whether that's really possible. For my part, I have questions about my own self-knowledge. But I know this much: If what I see or hear doesn't follow my own compass, it probably isn't right for me. Now, admittedly, different things affect different people in different ways. However, I've also seen too many people fail in my business because they bought lock, stock and barrel into what was supposed to be an aid for excellence in their field of endeavor.

Looking back 30 years, I recall very little coming out of companies in my field that I felt was helpful in the sales process. This doesn't mean that most of the "coaching" was harmful, just that it was too much surface and not enough depth—a mile wide and an inch deep: sales help, sales aids, sales congresses, sales meetings, etc. After looking at the countless reams of stuff that filtered down from the top, I concluded that most of the great ideas I ever received came from top salespeople, not top management people. The rest was pretty much useless, if not hurtful.

Along with misdirection from above, there's the computer. Twenty years ago I calculated it would bring the world to its economic knees by the year 2000. I may miss the target date, but the problem I perceive is not only predictable but inevitable. In the vital field of selling, the computer is a distraction for far too many whose primary job is to sell. It's also tied to an educational bureaucracy that produces countless college graduates with no place to go. Higher education is so preoccupied with computer-fed procedures and administrative foot-dragging that it cannot be made to recognize, for one staggering example, the need for an undergraduate degree in selling. I'll have a lot more to say on this remarkable deficiency later on.

To cut to the basics, I've functioned with two: building relationships and building a clientele. Day to day, nothing other than those two exercises is going to enhance sales. You do this by going face-to-face, one-by-one, every workday. You do *not* do it by poring over trade journals, crunching numbers out of a computer and then devoting more hours to fancy, computer-generated proposals. If you're a computer salesperson, obviously, you've got to know your product and be able to demonstrate how it works. But for the rest of us in the sales realm, computing and virtually everything else that delays or reduces direct, personal prospect/client contact is a sales liability—more so now than ever before. And the more drastically the business environment changes, the greater is the need to concentrate on that fundamental premise.

The Breakfast of (Sales) Champions

Routinely, I start my workday with a business breakfast, versus the colleague who munches down his coffee and Egg McMuffin alone, beats me to the office by half an hour, reads industry literature, hovers over a computer and otherwise blows the entire morning.

Meanwhile, I'm head to head with either a client or a *referred* prospect. (I always meet with someone by way of a referral, never through a cold call.) Let's say that, in this instance, I'm huddling for the first time with the president of a small company—perhaps 15 or 20 employees. I'll devote roughly the first hour of our conversation to uncovering his or her company problems.

There are several reasons for this take-it-easy approach: You don't come across as an impersonal order taker; you get to really know your prospect and what's bugging him or her; and you may be able to help, thereby maximizing your usefulness. It may sound incredible, but many times I've counseled a prospect for months on end before nailing down a penny's worth of sale. Conversely, that patience and helpfulness have frequently resulted in a multimillion dollar deal.

THE SECRET OF SERVICE

The operative word here is service—how you can help the person. More often than not, I'll be talking to a member of that mushrooming phenomenon, the entrepreneur. Happily, they're a dynamic, dedicated lot. But for all their energy and talent, they generally have very limited contacts beyond their own operations and are not versed in what an experienced, sympathetic salesperson can provide them. For example, they may not have a clue as to how their sales force should perform, other than to compare it with a somewhat similar operation. Or there may be a problem in delegating authority, which can be a fatal affliction. I've been delegating authority—empowering—since day one, so I'm in a good position to counsel on that score. And I can certainly address the underlying principles of a prospect's sales quotas. Granted, it takes time to garner the experience to enable such advising; so take your time. The point remains: Serve the client/prospect the best you can. The payoff will come in due course.

That isn't starry-eyed idealism, my friend. It's bare-bones practicality. The time-worn approach of pitching, signing and running is just that: time-worn—a prescription for career disaster. The old way is as dead as yesterday's news.

The point is illustrated by a recent entry in the comic strip "Blondie." In one panel, Blondie and Dagwood encounter a young fellow they hadn't seen in awhile. After exchanging pleasantries, they ask what the lad's been doing. In the next panel, he's reaching for a business card while informing them that he's selling insurance. The final panel reveals some swirls, indicating that Blondie and Dagwood ran away as fast as their feet could carry them. Nice image, right? Wrong! Plain awful! But justifiable?

That tarnished perception is aggravated by the failure in recent years of several major insurance companies. Faith has been shaken where trust and dollars had been invested. The inevitable, haunting question is "Can the company pay its claims?"

What we get down to is a matter of trust. It's what I've been striving for since that day I got married, at age 29, and since I made a commitment to build a strong clientele that would buy life insurance from me. I knew I couldn't do it with the proverbial ten cold calls a day, hoping to garner one sale—not when I correctly sensed I could turn that equation into nine victories out of ten direct, programmed contacts. My unique approach centered on great service, which included genuine helpfulness in solving clients' problems. People do not buy insurance so much as they buy people—or a concept.

It's amazing, really, how many people think business is conducted according to the price of a product. Cost is not in the thought process of the wealthy consumer who's buying a Lexus. Why buy a car? In my case, it's because I simply wanted to get from Point A to Point B—and I vowed never to buy a (then-priced) $10,000 Cadillac when I could drive around for one-fifth that amount. Luxury cars sell for reasons well beyond basic transportation, such as status, ego, etc. Not bucks.

Extravagance aside, the same applies to the woman buying a dress or the man buying a suit. The appeal of the garment, not the price, is what counts.

That's why, eventually, everything is sold, whether at sticker price or fire-sale cost. And, when you get down to the nitty-gritty, most of us have a tough time saying "No" to anybody. I love cookies. My wife makes them "from scratch," and they're superb. So what am I doing buying Girl Scout cookies? Certainly not because of quality or price. Those Girl Scout cookies are sold by the zillions because people want to support kids hustling on behalf of a worthy cause. The same goes for purchases of the $5 school candy bar, when you could get the same or better for a fraction of that amount. It applies to the lady doing her bit for the church bazaar. And a store can benefit immensely from a smiling, considerate cashier at a check-out counter (and suffer bankruptcy from a grouch).

We're in a people world, not a things world. Business goes where it's invited and remains where it's appreciated.

All of which brings us to this: The best method for selling is *face-to-face*. Not over a telephone. Not with letters to 1,000 prospective buyers. *Face-to-face*.

Some will argue that telecommunications eliminates such in-person contact—that all the fancy electronics "simplify" and "accelerate" and "modernize" the process.

Just remember that the word *phony* (i.e., fake) is derived from "telephone." The cold call is as unwelcome and impersonal as it is a reflection of sheer waste and human misery. Pity the poor drone who is required to telephone limitless numbers from a random list, day after day, using the same tired spiel. The pay is minimal. The rejection rate is astronomical. The job life expectancy can be measured in weeks at the outside. Ditto the miserable lot of the door-to-door salesperson who, barring the exceptional sufferer, is burned out within three months. Granted, a few people at the top of these horrible pyramids are making bucks. But they've thrown to the wolves legions of little guys and gals who shrug "It's a living" while sinking into substance abuse and strained or fractured family life. The lucky ones quit before they crack.

The prognosis is not all that much better for the sales novice who's been taught by a corporate management that couldn't sell a life raft to a drowning man. However, this is not the case with entrepreneurs, who, coincidentally, constitute the best sales force. Their operations are generally smaller and are headed mainly by sales pros. Rather than "educated bright," they are naturally bright, and their small size enables close daily contact and sales monitoring.

I don't mean to imply criticism of those who are trapped in big corporate sales training responsibilities. However, I've long since learned there are precious few among them with a successful sales background. It should be self-evident that one cannot teach what one has not learned, which is why more and more companies are going outside for assistance to broaden their approach to selling. Too many are long on systems and procedures, technical know-how and computerization, and short on selling.

Sales aspirants have been gulled into thinking that organization of a presentation, assembly of numbers, color-coding of lengthy proposals, etc., are essential to selling. But knowing a product is only 5 percent of the sales puzzle. The other 95 percent is knowing people and being willing to serve them; to invest a lot of listening to find out what the buyer wants or needs; to follow up regularly and consistently; and to work to convince your client to buy that second time around. This takes more than desire; it takes understanding of how to sell.

It does not take wining and dining prospects and clients constantly, or playing golf with them twice weekly. You may improve your golf game; it's unlikely you'll improve your business.

A salesperson can and should have a balanced life (which, unhappily, seems to be an endangered species in our break-neck society). And that is possible with a totally different approach to conventional selling.

THE QUEST FOR LEGITIMACY

My purpose here is to get you ready for what lies ahead. Long-range planning is needed—not simply six months or a year. You've got to gear up for the long haul. And the timing could not be better, because selling in our nation is in its embryonic stage. Hopefully it will become a profession, in the truest sense of that word. I've been awaiting such a development for a long time—since my early years, when I was told the professions were medical, legal and teaching. Selling was put down as a poor excuse for making a living.

But I firmly believe that selling can provide a beautiful life if you recognize that it is but one piece of the growing world of business. Companies are finally realizing, in tougher economic times, that they urgently need bright, well-educated, trainable, enthusiastic human beings. This means that appropriate treatment of productive salespeople is waiting in the wings.

Let me expand on that with this little scenario. Recently I served as consultant to a corporation that has a 26-person sales division, with an average income among them of $58,000 per year. The company wanted to know how it could do better. I asked these managers to identify their top salesperson. When they did, I placed an X, signifying the seller, at the upper-left corner of a blackboard. I continued with the X's, in descending order, according to each salesperson's proficiency. I then asked how much spread in sales there was between the highest- and lowest-ranked, and was told it was about five to one. Was the leader getting five times as much pay as the bottom of the barrel?, I inquired.

The reply was no—then the sheepish admission, "They both earned about the same." That inequity ended then and there; they knew they were vulnerable to losing a sales stemwinder—a person who spent the bulk of his time doing what he does best: selling. The ensuing step for management was to ask him how he does it. That's progress, and it's catching on—because it has to.

2

Pointers for Today

Moral discipline ultimately yields success. But there's a paradox here; success often corrupts moral discipline. Which is why I want to say, to young people especially, you'd better think long and hard about deciding between discipline or dependency.

Unfortunately, the option of dependency is frequently facilitated by parents who are as well-to-do as they are well-meaning. Wanting their children to "have a better life" than they had, they lavish their kids with instant gratification. Among the most miserable people I've ever met are those who always got everything (material) they ever wanted or wished for. You just cannot buy happiness or self-satisfaction. Those endlessly sought-after qualities must be earned. Sadly, they've become progressively threatened species.

WHEN TIMES WERE SIMPLER

In the days since the Great Depression through the late 1940s, the average employee had what I call good work units, which formed a foundation for pride in occupation. He worked comparatively longer hours and days for a paycheck that may barely have met the family's basic needs. There wasn't much wish-list money left over. Tragically, many who yearned to work could not find employment. Most wouldn't take a government dole; they were too proud and too ashamed to reach for a handout.

In the big factories, management and an emerging labor force slugged it out for benefits that have long since been taken for granted (although there has been substantial slippage lately in fringe packages). On the other hand, at the smaller shops and offices, the 1930s and 1940s were years of respectful relationships between bosses and employees. They formed teams to concentrate on collectively doing their best.

In contrast, we've been paying the competition-losing price for an attitude summarized in the phrase, "It's good enough." Not the best; just what you can get by with. Since the 1950s, the pattern has been one of higher pay for lower quality—a philosophy based in laziness that says, "No one will ever notice [the deficiencies]." But people *did* notice. Enter Honda, Toyota, Mitsubishi, Canon, Nissan, Matsushita and all the others who've been eating our lunch right off our own table.

The media, of course, played a role in the erosion of our national spirit. Have "the good life." "The best part of waking up is Folger's in your cup." (Funny, but I always thought the best part of waking up is ... waking up!) Daily, we're inundated with the notion that the livin' ought to be easy. and have you noticed the number of support groups outside the family? The family used to provide the support of its members because the family unit was strong. Father knew best. Mother partnered in running the kingdom. The kids listened, acted accordingly, or else. Talks around the kitchen table didn't want or need the substitute of a psychiatrist's couch. Weaken the family unit and the members fan out with "help wanted" signs, craving assistance for every imaginable affliction.

Greed is certainly one of those afflictions. I read recently where the CEO of a (decidedly unnecessary) soft drink company received an annual paycheck of $56 million. What could one person possibly do with all that loot? Tell you what *I* think he could do: spread half of it around to his employees. They'd consider him a hero, and he wouldn't even notice the difference. Would you feel neglected if your pay were $28 million instead of $56 million? Of course not—especially if your "denial" helped salvage some jobs.

And job salvaging—retention and creation—has to be the top priority. Society deserves a productive return on the welfare provided to able-bodied recipients; that should be a given. But equally important, recipients need the uplifting boost and dignity that go with working, being productive and accomplishing something that's worthwhile. I'm truly convinced that people *need* to work for their own well-being, let alone society's.

HUMANS: ON THE ROAD TO OBSOLESCENCE?

As for the army of workers being pink-slipped, it's the hallmark of a revolution evolution. Man had progressed from the agrarian to the industrial. Those progressions were comparatively snail-paced when you consider the sudden impact of the computer and its high-tech–era relatives. Sure, the computer is a marvel . . . like the 800-pound gorilla on the loose. Kids are lining up by the mile to learn its secrets—in reality, like lemmings headed toward the sea. Where legions of humans were once needed to make a factory hum, a computer and a couple pairs of hands can now do the whole thing more precisely. And I'm not simply referring to blue-collar workers, either. Check what's been happening—and is in store—for the white collars in the Fortune 500-plus crowd. Decimation (one in ten eliminated) is too mild a term; it's more like "slaughter." One of these years I expect, only half-kiddingly, that GM will crank out nine million cars with a ten-person work force. But there won't be any buyers because of runaway unemployment.

And, from a technological standpoint, the script seems to get wilder and wilder. For instance, we're on the brink of something even more dramatic than Henry Ford's introduction of mass-produced automobiles: mass-produced solar panels to capture the sun's power, opening the way to cheap electricity. Goodbye oil, nuclear, gas, coal; hello solar panels and rock-bottom utility bills. Not so fast; there's still no such thing as a free lunch. In the wake of our sailing toward a revolutionary electric charge, many another job will be washed ashore.

Nor do I think it prudent to rely on government to make up the difference—at least not on its own. One hard look at the latest presidential election race and you've got to squirm about whether politics dictates economics or vice versa. In any event, we're still passing out "protection" billions to the Russians, et al.—so much that I'd think the Russians would be tempted to point their guns at their own heads instead of ours. Meanwhile, we just keep piling up debt, $1 trillion upon another. Somebody's gotta pay. And, as Pogo used to put it, "We have met the enemy, and he is us."

I'm neither Solomon nor a futurist; I'm more a logician, I guess. On that score, I think we have another decade of recession ahead of us, and an inevitable depression. The latter will not be an unmitigated disaster. For one thing, rampant crime should subside. You can't rob people who have next to nothing in cash or other valuables. Backyard gardens will reappear, as much to salvage mental health as to put food on tables. Perhaps in place of the high-tech madness we'll get some high touch—a greater sensitivity toward our fellow humans and a reinvigorated sense of personal responsibility and self-reliance.

When I was in my twenties, I worked simultaneously as a butcher, coach, teacher and insurance salesman. When I got married, I was as close to being flat broke as I could be. But I never even thought of asking for help in trying to put together a business or for any other purpose. In those days, the mental environment was such that, sonny boy, if you want to survive in the jungle, you'd better accept the fact that you'll do it on your own. Bluntly, nobody else cares. That's the way it was; that's the way it ought to be. It was a hard, no-give discipline. But I wouldn't have wanted it any other way.

Time out. I've been laying some heavy gloom-and-doom stuff on you. Even with the disclaimers that a depression has silver-lining potential, that it could be the catalyst for sorting things out, for regaining lost virtues, etc., no sane person wants the suffering a depression imposes. I just think it's going to happen.

So where does this leave you? (I'm too old and too secure to worry about a worst-case senario. I'm also assuming most readers of this book are salespeople of a younger age, or are contemplating a career in sales.) Well, take heart. You can still make it, irrespective of the economy over the next 20 years. Success in selling is in direct proportion to effort. You won't have to worry about legislation that could eliminate your job, or about a computer eliminating an entire floor of employees. Sales is the one profession that will be ever-expanding, because the practitioner will have creativity, a high degree of enthusiasm and a willingness to invest whatever time is needed. Tied to a reasonably good income, most people in sales enjoy a wealth of freedom—the capacity to divide their work hours as they see fit. You cannot beat the combination. And the result is usually happiness.

3

Thinking People and Action People

I'd heard the old expression long ago: Actions speak louder than words. I've always been intrigued by what that saying implies. In other words, what happens in the selling interview—to the salesperson, to the buyer—indeed, in the whole world of sales? My simplistic conclusion: After all is said and done, more is said than done.

Helping me reach that conclusion was the input from an old friend, George Aberl, a representative of Connecticut Mutual. When we were young and trying to establish ourselves as insurance agents, I'd drop by after work every couple of weeks or so to visit with George, just to kick things around, like sales procedures and what we both were going through.

One night, out of the blue, George opined that most people are thinking people or action people. It was a new one on me, so I asked him to elaborate. He did, for about 15 minutes, ending with the expressed hope that I would get a better insight into myself. Then came his capper: "John, you're the only one I've ever met who is both a thinking person and an action person." I took it as a compliment, although any credit would have to be spread far beyond whatever I may have invested to earn George's evaluation—family, religion, teachers.

What George did for me was to open a panoramic view of what I was about. Maybe I can help do the same for you—spark an insight into your thinking and action capabilities. Briefly, regardless of a person's intellectual skills and no matter how long he or she may want to indulge in mental gymnastics, the time comes when action must or should be taken.

That axiom brings to mind a story concerning arguably the world's greatest operatic singer, Enrico Caruso. One night, a covey of critics sought to account for his world renown. One suggested it was due to an industrious advance man who was a genius at handling all the arrangements, publicity and promotion. Another credited Caruso's insistence on performing only in the finest theatres. Still another linked the singer's fame to the accompaniment of 100 violinists—an unprecedented musical assemblage. Then it came to the oldest critic's turn, who'd been listening attentively to his colleagues. He said he agreed with all of them. Then he added the punch line: "But remember, there comes that time every evening when Caruso must sing."

That was a mouthful. A' la Caruso, there's a time when the athlete must leave the locker room; it's called game time. To the salesperson more inclined toward thinking than acting: You must take that God-given talent and convert it into effective communication, in front of a prospective buyer. That's the action part. You put it off at your peril.

DEALING WITH FEAR OF REJECTION

But that meshes completely with my long-held contention that there is more caller reluctance (fear of rejection) than has ever been written about. Maybe a little yarn a friend told me at a meeting in Canada will help put that fear into perspective. Here's the setting: A guy and his dog are relaxing together at home. Doorbell rings. Pooch races to the door. Know what? The caller did not come to see the dog. Ten minutes later, doorbell rings again. Zoom! Off runs Fido to bark a greeting. Same result. Nobody ever comes to see the dog. Yet the mutt has learned to handle it. Every time that doorbell rings, he's off and running. Sure, he's a lot more active than thoughtful. But the point is, that dog learned to accept rejection with vim, vigor and vitality. We can learn from man's best friend.

Most people in our business see one prospect a day, maximum, in a selling interview. What can be done to stimulate more action? I say the stimulus is needed in both thinking and action categories. We have many intellectual types who can think themselves into oblivion. It's like the top graduate who settles for being a perpetual student, never venturing forth from the ivory tower. There are those in our business who have a slew of degrees but who cannot bring themselves to jump out of the trenches and engage in hand-to-hand "combat." To be sure, academic accomplishment deserves our applause. Really great thinkers will always be in great demand. But without action, things just cannot shake and move. Contemplating one's navel or speculating on how many angels can dance on the head of a pin may be pleasant and/or fascinating, but neither will produce a seller, a buyer, an income or a profit.

Remember when you were in school, evaluating teachers, sorting through academic materials, trying to match them up with your objectives? Now that you're out of college and into the game of selling, that school-age sifting and probing probably hasn't changed all that much. The difference comes in pondering all manner of things in one's professional life, but not knowing when to act. Being too preoccupied with avoiding risks. Waiting for the perfect situation, where the only answer to the sales pitch is "yes." Being glued to a desk, churning numbers, evaluating proposals, reviewing, procrastinating, dreading the seller/prospect confrontation.

Yet dialogue between practitioner and prospect is the ultimate in thinking/action. I happen to love it. When your part of the dialogue incorporates a burning desire to serve the prospect, that *has* to be felt. Motivation of that magnitude cannot be hidden or ignored. Genuine, helpful motivation reveals two people interested in what is being discussed. And that degree of motivation lies within each of us, often waiting to be discovered. I teach, but I cannot motivate another person. I can only motivate myself and then try to unlock the door for my audience, or student, or buyer. There are no standardized methods that can be applied here. But what can be put into effect instantaneously is a greater understanding of how you work, how you think and what you do with your thinking to bring it down to simple communication for the benefit of the buyer. If you can manage that introspection, I guarantee that your prospect will take action. Recognize that there is only one legitimate reason that a person does not buy what you are selling: He or she does not have the money to make the purchase. The fortunate flip side to selling is that you can always go to someone who does have the money for a buy.

If good prospects (people with money) are not buying from you, examine your methods and the thinking behind them. Are you truly interested in the welfare of the prospect? If you think you pass the tests, especially the one involving true interest in your prospects, and if you continue to add to your knowledge in the field, you will be a welcome surprise to the other thinking person who is waiting for motivation to buy from you.

4

Skills for Selling and for Living

In an earlier chapter, I cited statistics on the number of professional salespeople plying their trade in the United States. To those I added nonprofessional sellers—kids swapping baseball cards, FSBOs (for sale by owner . . . of almost anything imaginable or salable), garage sales, bake sales. Then there are the additional countless numbers who sell ideas (clergy, instructors, politicians, military strategists and tacticians) and the troops who carry out their plans. Briefly, we're all in sales, or sales management, with the managers selling their methods to their respective sales forces so they can be successful in marketing or projecting their common product. A step deeper and we find we're all in the "people business," the exercise of relating to each other for either a tangible or intangible exchange or transaction.

As in every endeavor involving human beings, you're bound to lose some along the way. The impossible goal is to win every time. It can't be done; but the goal is well worth retaining as a measure against the degree of success or failure. The best of hopes is to win more than you lose, year after year.

THE ULTIMATE SALE

Regardless of one's religious orientation (even for those without any), the life of Jesus Christ offers a peerless example of the "sales" phenomenon, with all its attendant victories and defeats. Christ assumed an extraordinarily difficult challenge: selling eternal salvation to the self-indulgent, to the unbelieving, to those who adored all sorts of other gods. Yet He carried a message that more and more people came to listen to: the concept of a single, loving heavenly Father and the promise of an "afterlife." For the multitudes who cried, "Is this all there is [to life]?," Christ could respond soothingly, "No, there's much more; you *can* be with Me in paradise."

But to save people, Christ had to bring to them His message. And not by direct mail solicitation. Even if there had been a thoroughgoing postal service in His time—along with fax machines, telephone banks and similar doo-dads—I'm sure that, from the outset, Christ would have taken the direct, eyeball-to-eyeball approach. He also availed Himself of an intercedent, in the form of John the Baptist. Christ the unknown introduced by John the known. (I'll pause momentarily here to reiterate some salient points: Good sellers do not make cold calls; they never use anything other than face-to-face contact; they always initiate contact from a referral.) Christ recognized the fallacy in trying to convince the masses that He was good. John the Baptist served that vital introductory purpose—a referral from a respected source.

Similarly, Christ went one-on-one in recruiting His apostles. He didn't send them a résumé and an elaborate treatise on papyrus. Then, after He'd educated them in the portent of His message, He sent them onto the highways and byways, as advance men, if you will, to prepare the way for the Lord.

Many listened to the Supreme Salesman, and many converted to Christianity: Christ's satisfied customers—so satisfied in the faith He sold and they bought that they went resolutely, even happily, to their deaths by persecution. However, even the greatest seller of the greatest of messages experienced heart-rending rejection and betrayal, and from His innermost circle. Judas sold out for 30 pieces of silver. Peter denied Him not once but three times. Thomas, after all the miracles he'd seen or heard about, expressed doubts. And Christ's earthly epitaph was nailed to the cross on which he was crucified. Christ knew what was coming. He knew the human factor, and that He would be constantly confronted by it.

Can that human factor ever be overcome? Christ's example contains the obvious answer: a cold and irreversible NO! And yet His word survives 2,000 years later—an absolutely mind-boggling accomplishment, unmatched by any other endeavor. There have been slippages in Christianity, to be sure. But there's always been recovery and renewal, ebbs and flows—as in life at large or in one's career. But no setback will defeat the truly committed, whether it's converting heathens or recruiting clients. It's still "people selling to people," with its highs and lows, elation and depression. Nothing is perfect; never was, never will be. The trick lies in recognizing and accepting those truisms. It'll make the inevitable hard knocks easier to absorb, and recovery faster.

UNIQUE STYLES ARE KEY TO SALES SUCCESS

I've certainly had my ups and downs in 40 years of selling. I've seen virtual armies of salespeople who had a very rough go and quit in utter discouragement. That bothers me a lot, because on the whole, I've had it comparatively easy. And I don't see why that kind of experience has not been distributed more universally. My first book was title. *The Easy Sale,* implying my methodology for selling. For the sake of happier salespeople, I'd like to see more converted to my method, as well as to the principles espoused in my last book, *High Touch Selling* (as opposed to high tech). The common thread between the two books is something I recognized from the most successful sellers I've met: They are truly intriguing because they are *different* from other sellers. They developed their own unique way to sell. So did I. So should you.

Feel free to borrow anything or everything I've laid before you, be it speech or book. Incidentally, I've found writing a book to be anything but fun. The fun comes after it's written. Writing isn't my real game; selling is. And I enjoy selling immensely, even though there isn't a day that goes by that I don't have at least a couple of "down" times.

But I know they're coming and I know how to put them in perspective, put them aside and get on with the business at hand—office, home, wherever. Also—and unlike my hero, Christ—I know I don't have to sacrifice my life for my message.

The Value of Fiscal Responsibility

But while all of us hurt to varying degrees as we go from day to day, so much of it is self-inflicted pain. In the realm of personal finances, where inadequacy breeds so many individual and family miseries, there is mounting evidence of disregard, if not outright contempt, for setting aside the proverbial nest-egg. As one who has emphasized the importance of savings, I remain appalled at how little is saved. Discipline has flown the coop. In its stead we've gone from "conspicuous consumption" to whatever cute buzzword represents the same pattern. Money follows advertising bombardments like rats following the Pied Piper. Plastic credit—and blank minds—has been sucked into buying luxury cars, overpriced homes, designer clothes and a whole slew of expensive, frivolous toys for kids who want to emulate their profligate parents. Give yourself one of the most reassuring breaks in the material world: Restrain yourself long enough each month to put some money aside for the rainy day you *know* is coming. Then do the same for your clients. First, it's for your own protection. Second, you won't form much of an impression on a financial management/insurance prospect when word gets around that you've spent yourself to the cleaners. Third, your success in getting clients to save over the long haul is one of the finest services you can provide them. It goes hand-in-hand with peace of mind—theirs and yours.

Time and the Work Ethic

Then, get organized! I've never seen a good salesperson who operated without solid organization. Know how to maximize the value of your hours and minutes. Recognize the nonsense in the whine, "Oh, if only

I had more time." Or, "Let George do it; he has more time." Crybabies are just that: immature gripers. They cannot admit that there is no such thing as more time; we're all given the same amount, year-round. We all waste time. The question is, how much? You can't fool the second hand of a clock. It keeps on rolling around and around. Ask yourself, are too many seconds being frittered away?

That question dovetails with another critical phase in getting organized—i.e., the work ethic. It's peeling away like paint in a flophouse—including in my own organization. Recently, a new secretary in our shop had the temerity to stop me when I was leaving to impart what, for her, was an unsettling observation: "All Lisa and Wilma [my secretaries] do is work!" Rough translation: Most of the secretaries don't work as hard as my secretaries. I recovered sufficiently to respond to this quasi-complaint that working is the reason they were hired. Poor old Ben Franklin and his little homily about a busy man being a happy man. Now, it seems, "happiness" is gleaned from discussing the coming weekend, next vacation, who's dating whom, ball scores, trivial pursuits. Perhaps we're dealing here with a distortion of terms. The dividend may be (ephemeral) pleasure; it is *not* happiness. That comes from accomplishment. And career accomplishment cannot come without a fair amount of work. If you're effectively organized to do your job, chances are you'll feel good about yourself at the end of the day. *That's* happiness.

And try to avoid the abyss of self-deception. When you're reviewing your personal organization, evaluate your skills, what you're doing, how you're doing and what you want to do. As you should not be too rough on yourself, don't be too patronizing, either. In a word, be honest and candid. Many a military commander has bitten the dust—and carried legions of unfortunates with him—because he thought he could "fool the troops." Sooner or later, the fallacy is penetrated by yourself or others.

Keep Your Image in Focus

To extend that line, consider these broad groupings and your relationship to them:

- What you want others to think you are
- What others think you are
- What you think you are
- What you are

Your hope should be to get the four elements as close to reality as you're able. And then remember to laugh—at yourself and with others. Seriously, it's one of the best therapies around. It's medically documented that laughter is good for the body. And there's so much wisdom in the timeless expression, "Laugh and the world laughs with you; cry and you cry alone." The influence of a sourpuss is as infectious as bubonic plague. So is a two-legged ray of sunshine.

Remember the Mission

What you do not want to concern yourself with when in an organizing mode is the element of control. Quick little story: At a corporate board meeting I attended, one of the managers said, "I think I'm losing control of one of the executives in my division." My reaction: "You never have to worry about *losing* control if you do not control others." Point: Controlling *yourself* is the only legitimate concern. What about leadership and control? They have nothing in common. The true leader understands that most of his or her ideas come from others. The mission is to lead, not control. The difference is cavernous. There's a library full of books on sales leadership. Any reasonably intelligent salesperson can read the chapter titles and be able to perform his or her own personal evaluation according to the principles we've just examined.

A MODERN LOOK AT OLD-FASHIONED VALUES

There are also some other principles, ones you're not likely to find in the sales how-to texts, leadership or otherwise. I'm talking about morality and integrity, and I do so without squirming one tiny bit. The subjects are overripe for comment. Our society has been going to hell in a handbasket because of the indulgence of spouses who cheat on each other and then burden their children and society with a fractured family. Guy signs a contract for millions, breaks the contract for more millions—and no penalty. Half the kids born are illegitimate; fat chance they're given. Failed S&Ls reflect an unparalleled myopia of greed. From the Capitol to Wall Street and coast to coast, dishonesty is the password.

What a far cry from the story of the worker whose chore it was to climb to the top of a steeple and pound 500 nails into boards he knew full well nobody else would examine. He pounded in 499 nails straight as arrows, then bent the last one. He could have called it quits ("Who'd know the difference?") and gone home. But he extracted the errant nail and banged in a new and straight one. Integrity. I want that kind of person to be my doctor, my lawyer, my car mechanic, my painter, my friend. Don't you feel the same way about those upon whom you depend? Doesn't your client? Or would you prefer a Michael Milken, or an Ivan Boesky, or one of similar ilk? I'm sure we'd all like to put our money on that honest carpenter.

I didn't actually see that carpenter, but I'd bet he never let himself get suckered into the "dress for success" crowd, either. I shared a speakers' platform with the fellow who coined that term, and heard him extol the merits of wearing $900 suits. I felt like throwing up. Forget the fact that my wife has to remind me to comb my hair, or that I'd make a super-expensive suit look like a hand-me-down within a few hours. I'm not into trying to impress people with my wardrobe, and I feel sorry for anyone who is—especially a salesperson who has to earn a living. Spending an inordinate amount of time on personal appearance equates to horribly misplaced priorities; superficiality to a skin-depth degree; time and money grossly misspent. As long as you're neat, your clients aren't going to be concerned about your jacket, tie, shoes, car—unless it's obvious you're working overtime at them and not using that time to serve the people whose trust you need.

Instead of "dress for success" silliness, I think we could do with more reminders on being compassionate. Compassion—really caring about people—fits like a glove with a good work ethic, being happy and being successful. Successful not like a Donald Trump, but like a Mother Theresa. Hey, I'm no saint or anything near what that marvelous nun represents. Nor do I expect it of others. By the same token, I do want to see substantial improvements in my chosen profession. And such improvement has got to be tied to an integrity guided by the Golden Rule. Treat the other guy and gal the way you'd like them to treat you (me). It's so simple and so beautiful. I guess that's why it's so elusive. Getting it back in vogue could do an awful lot in helping to stem the deterioration swamping us from all sides.

5

Discipline and Spirituality

What, you may well ask, do these subjects have to do with a book written primarily for salespeople?

My answer: not a little, not a lot. Everything!

Without self-discipline, I sincerely believe it is not possible to be happy—that is, to love and to be loved in return, to share joys, to feel good about oneself, to get the best out of what is often a trying existence under the best of circumstances.

Without spirituality, it's possible to be successful in one sense of the word; for example, the person who has no religious base but who has uncompromising scruples as well as the capacity to do unto others as he would have them do unto him. But, for all of that, I think that spirituality fills a mighty void that cannot be filled by any other source. It can console when nothing else can. It can accommodate what reason cannot explain. It can elevate one beyond what often appears to be incredible cruelty and senseless misery, above the repeated instances of bad things happening to good people. I am, of course, talking about genuine spirituality, founded in a sincere faith that governs one's behavior. It is not a weekly exercise in socializing—the kind that allows the rules of faith to be dismissed the moment the "worshipper" exits the church, synagogue or mosque. That is an exercise in self-deception and hypocrisy. And discipline and spirituality can and should be mutually supportive, as well as their own reward.

Forget for a moment the application of discipline and spirituality to the individual. Look at them in the context of our nation. Our moral foundations have been under siege for years.

A SOCIETY IN DECLINE

Never was this more apparent than when the term "Me generation" was coined. What a telling way to capsulize the character of a citizenry spanning 20-odd years. It denotes a preoccupation with pleasure-seeking, even to the extent of splitting married couples at the drop of a hat; legions of babies born without fathers to rear them; and/or abortion on demand. Sexually transmitted diseases have exploded in really frightening proportions. Runaway debt has been fueled in large measure by greed-driven lenders subsidizing foolish projects demanded by irresponsible borrowers. Crime has skyrocketed, thanks in no small measure to a coast-to-coast addiction to drugs and liquor. Leveraged corporate buyouts have been perpetrated by highly educated manipulators who didn't give a thought to the legions who were thrown out of work and into the abyss of despair. Because of profligate behavior, the very water we drink, the air we breathe and the land we traverse are in dire straits. As we pollute our environment, so do we pollute our children: Suicide is now the number-one killer among teenagers. Is this the bill for "progress" or the reflection of a disciplined, spiritual nation? And are we happier as a people?

My unequivocal answer is an emphatic no. We're paying the price as a society because we haven't paid the price as individuals. Discipline and spirituality/morality are not only not irritants, inconveniences or qualities to be otherwise "suffered," they are the highways to individual and societal quality of life. To me, the restrictions imposed by discipline and spirituality are anything but nuisances; they are irrevocably in *my best interests*. They *improve* my life materially and philosophically, at every level and with whomever I encounter. I want and need the limitations these qualities impose upon me because I recognize that without them, I'd be an unmitigated flop in every phase of my life that's worth the time of day.

I stress this theme to demonstrate how trying to be disciplined and moral works for the practitioner. What does discipline entail? Where does it come from? Well, I don't agree with the stance that discipline comes from within. I say it's a learned attribute, injected from the outside, to be polished throughout one's life.

A POWERFUL EXAMPLE

I got my "injection" from an iron-fisted, deeply religious father. To him, discipline carried no latitude. As the eldest son, I was first in line for a comeuppance. But every time I felt his wrath, I knew I deserved it. I also knew that nobody exhibited more self-discipline than my dad. And I thank God that he did, because he was so sorely tried. My mother died during the birth of their ninth child. Dad could have farmed some of us out to other relatives without fear of recriminations. After all, the brood was very large, and he did have a horrendously tough grocery business to juggle, to say nothing of trying to suppress his immeasurable grief. Instead, he stuck out that fierce Irish jib and vowed we'd all stick together. It wasn't easy, but with dad calling the shots, we made it. He literally disciplined himself to live for others—primarily for his kids. When he died, he did so in the incomparable knowledge that he single-handedly had left me with eight wonderful sisters and brothers, followed by a wave of beautiful grandchildren. He died an unqualified success; he died happy. Discipline and spirituality—from an unparalleled role model.

It took me awhile, but I did get around to polishing the self-discipline to which my dad had introduced me. It finally began sinking in: Discipline is *control* of oneself. Not drudgery, not the hallmark of a Spartan or prudish mentality, but a real asset for personal gain and a better life. Increasingly, I wanted to control my actions and reactions. So to me, remaining in control meant not drinking alcoholic beverages. I'm not against drinking, per se; the love of my life has an occasional "pop." It's just that booze is a behavioral modifier I neither want nor need. Besides, I've never had a hangover or even a close approximation of one. (Pals joke that I'll never know what it's like to feel better as the day progresses because I'll never know what it's like to pull out of a liquor-laced fog.)

Taking charge of my actions/reactions enables me to say that in 33 years of marriage, I've never had a single argument with my wife. Honest Injun! True, I married a saint, which sure has helped. But I've also appreciated that you don't have to be a wimp to concede a point, to back off from what could develop into a spat, to absorb a few mental blows or to just keep your mouth shut. It starts with: I love her more than my next breath. If Kate calls me at the office, I drop everything to find out what she wants. I know she won't call me unless she thinks it's important. If she thinks it's important, it's important to me. Any flea-brain can play macho-man. But who wins in that sort of idiot contest? Me, I've won every single day of 33 years.

THE STRENGTH OF FAMILY FOUNDATIONS

My devotion to Kate and to discipline grew together. Before I was married, I was a classic spendthrift. But when we walked down the aisle, knowing we both wanted a large family—and had all of $180 in the bank after our honeymoon—we determined to save one-half my income our first five years together. Unavoidably, having babies in rapid succession (the first three within less than three years) was going to take some bucks. And, ever the disciplinarian, my dad never asked if I needed financial assistance. To him it was simple: You want it, then suit up and go after it.

I convinced myself I had no desire or impulse to spend beyond what really needed to be spent. Kate never worked outside the home, never wanted to. But she's worked inexhaustibly at home, first in a small, walk-up apartment, eventually in a house big enough to hold seven sons, two daughters, mother, father and occasional visitors. She's always cooked "from the ground up," done all of her own housecleaning, tutored the children—everything. All I did was bring home the bacon, or anything else she said she needed. (We're now in a smaller but still spacious house.) Kate still does everything involving homemaking.

If I went to a ball game (the only recreation that interests me), it was usually admission-free because I was an ex-coach. In those early years, the only times I paid to get in was to see the University of Toledo play. And I bought no hot dogs, either for me or, later on, for the kids. Denied hot dogs, the kids were learning that you don't get everything in life you *want*. Need is something else.

Growing up, they learned that dinner would involve roughly an hour and a half of everybody's time, all of us together. Dinner was for food and lots of dialogue. If mom or dad were late, they were to just keep talking things over until everyone could assemble. After dinner, there was no TV; just three hours of studying.

When they went to college (eight graduates thus far; one post-graduate attorney, another converting from a business degree to become a doctor), it was with the understanding that they'd pay half the cost, refundable upon graduation. With the boys, there was no problem. Of the two girls, Kelly landed a major athletic scholarship, also no problem. But Patty ran into the high hurdle of the low-paying jobs available to young women. Plucky kid, she tried her best. But that meant working an 8:30 p.m. to 4 a.m. shift. After some sleepless nights awaiting her safe arrival, it dawned on us that this was a pretty dumb arrangement. So Patty paid for her books and clothes, we paid the tuition. Sure, I could have easily paid for everything upfront; I'd been making big money for years. But giving them a clear trip from the start would have deprived them of the discipline and self-esteem that goes with earning their way, of struggling to reach their goal. We love our kids too much to ever let them believe that life is just a bowl of cherries. They've succeeded thus far in their young lives—that is, they're happy. Discipline works. And Kate and I are satisfied they're going to want their children to fully appreciate that clearest of truths.

I'll admit I've slipped time and again on the discipline score. As with Patty's case, it's silly to resist an adjustment when one is clearly called for. But my admission isn't about being stoically inflexible and then making a reasonable change. I just plain goof off. One of my most glaring failures lies in neglecting to follow through on cleaning up my desk. Constantly I swear to never let the beast get ahead of me, only to see that I've done just that—and then tear into a sprucing that should have been done two or three weeks previously. So, I'm human. But (and here's the key) I don't give up trying. I know the inevitable, unwelcome consequences that await me if I don't shape up.

Let me also be the first to admit that I've been uncommonly blessed, all the discipline in the world notwithstanding. I could have lost my beautiful wife, or been incapacitated, or suffered any of the scores of permanent setbacks that can afflict any of us. That's why I'm so grateful, and also deeply touched by the true heroism of those who struggle to overcome the situation where both parents feel obligated to work, or who are the single head of household. I know magnificent people in both camps—and in the poorest of neighborhoods. Often, they must rely on only themselves to be the role models for their children.

These people deserve all the help we can give them. One of various ways I've sought to lend such a hand has been in sponsoring, for 22 years straight, summer sports camps for some 400 deserving children. There they learn more about basketball, and are taught various character-building skills by exemplary coaches. I'll never forget the positive impressions I absorbed as a young man from being around Monsignor Jerome Schmitt. My father aside, the good monsignor was the greatest mentor of my life, and I was blessed with many memorable mentors. I've long since believed that one person can, if not turn around a life, certainly make an enormous difference in one. If just one of those 400 summer camp kids per year got a character-building lift from one of the coaches I hired, the cost has been one of the best investments I could ever make. Kids would not be tagged "underprivileged" if more of us who have been privileged gave them some love and attention. That's why I'm also committed to helping provide instruction and counseling at an inner-city school. It's a challenge I relish, and I believe deep down that this brand-new undertaking will make a difference in a lot of kids' lives. And that's the purpose behind the effort.

The impetus for that project is spiritual in nature. Instead of a paycheck, I anticipate getting a "gracecheck." Grace: a spiritual dividend that goes with doing something for the other guy. The size of the dividend is determined by what you do and how you do it. I'll derive more from this task because I'm contributing *myself* as opposed to merely writing a check for the proverbial worthy cause.

Over the years I've put a lot of money and personal exertion into charities of numerous stripes. If my wife precedes me in death, I hope, when my time comes to join her, that I wind up with no more than $1 in my pocket. Every year I progressively crank up the amount of money I contribute to and for others. As with self-control, it's a selfish thing. I'm happier, and feel better, when I exercise my spiritual side.

Although I was born and raised a Catholic, I have the utmost respect for those of other faiths who endeavor to live by their respective credos. Their foundations are related in that they honor God and promulgate love of man. The more love, the less travail. What's heartbreaking is the way man can twist religion (and its close relative, ethnicity) into an excuse for killings and wars.

I'll pray until the day I check out for the last time. I recommend spirituality to every living person. For me, it's made for a satisfying life beyond any reckoning. Spirituality/discipline, like Siamese twins, are complementary and self-sustaining. They work; they're needed.

6

Service Means Sales

As I observe our society, the most important aspect I find fast eroding in almost every field of endeavor is that of service. Indeed, quality service is becoming so rare that the public is virtually stunned when it is encountered. This helps explain why

- many businesses suddenly find themselves in a slump.
- consumers flit from one product line to another.
- the rarity of good service generates repeat business.

People will happily, eagerly return to those who give them special treatment.

Yet what do we encounter from one day to the next? Whether I'm having breakfast at a well-known restaurant, picking up some milk on the way home or taking the family out for a pizza, I'm left with the feeling that the businesses I'm patronizing couldn't care less if I passed them by. But the *investors* in those businesses care. They want my dollars, and those of anyone else they can snare, on a repeat basis. But that attitude has not been conveyed with any degree of success or consistency by the people who count most, the troops on the line—the ones who effect the sale. That's why the seller who leaps that hurdle, who knows the importance of providing good service all the time, is ahead of the competition and well along the road to sales effectiveness.

Of course, it's management's responsibility to reward such an effective individual with appropriate income, latitude and recognition. No really productive salesperson, who generates repeat business routinely, is going to remain loyal to an insensitive or miserly employer. Loyalty is a two-way street. If it isn't running in one direction, it won't run in the other.

So if there's deficiency in service, we have deficient servants. Historically, the servant served the master. Today, instead of feudal lords and ladies, the client is the master. That client may not hold the literal power of life or death over the servant, but he or she can figuratively kill the inattentive salesperson just as effectively as a guillotine.

THE ANNUAL CLIENT REVIEW

To illustrate the extent of my devotion to the service side of selling as it pertains to my operation, let me tune you into a conversation I shared during the first month of this book's preparation. It occurred at my office during an impromptu, casual gathering of four people: two sales colleagues; my invaluable secretary, Wilma; and me. Out of the blue, Wilma was asked what she considered to be the most important ingredient in my success as a salesman. Without batting an eye, Wilma responded, "The annual client review." This lady knows every minute of my schedule, follows or processes every word of my correspondence and has a total overview of everything my business hopes to accomplish. Without Wilma and my other secretary, Lisa, I'd be in Never-Never Land. So when she said annual client review was most responsible for my generating sales, she spoke from a mother lode of experience—and I think she hit the nail right on the head.

Annual client review is precisely what the phrase implies. Within a given year, I make it an absolute mandate to try to meet with every one of my clients—richest to poorest, blue collar to top executive. Generally it's at my office, not at their home or workplace. I do this to "just keep in touch"—find out what or how they're doing, exhibit my interest and concern for their lives and update them on changes and trends that can be of timely value.

In round numbers, at the height of my business I was dealing with, say, 1,000 clients. Now it's roughly 900, reduced by 53 deaths and a similar number of client relocations, as well as a planned cutback in my workload.

The 80/20 Ratio

What is the inherent value of annual client reviews? Let me tick off a few bits of evidence: 80 percent of my productivity comes from 20 percent of my policyholders—and it is beyond predicting which 20 percent it will be one year to the next. Give or take a few, those contacts will spawn 40 referrals that otherwise would not have materialized had I not conducted the reviews.

On the point of not knowing who among that valuable clientele will be the source of unexpected revenues: In 1957 I sold a $5,000 policy to a gentleman who today has a $1 million policy—that from a fellow whose financial growth had been even less predictable than my own, which was totally unpredictable.

In the hallway discussion referred to earlier, Wilma, after expressing her perplexity at why every salesperson does not have yearly client reviews, pointed out that on that very day three of my client interviews had initiated applications for additional coverage. One felt his wife needed more coverage; another wanted to know whether he could roll a bank IRA into an annuity; the third sought to increase an existing annuity. I was happy to oblige on all scores. (For those who may be puzzled by an annuity inside an IRA that already has a tax-deferred standing, you should know that our annuity was paying 8 percent while the IRA was paying 5 percent.) The critical point is that three of the six people I'd seen up to that part of the day—one-half—were annual review clients who provided me with more business. According to Wilma's estimate, that was part of a pattern that, in fewer than four months, had produced as many as 30 sales out of a total year-to-date volume of 129. On a case basis, that equates to 20–25 percent of the total being attributable to the reviews, or 60–70 new sales a year from customers revealing their needs, plus an additional 30 or so evolving from my input or recommendations. That flies in the face of the conventional "wisdom" that the salesman is traditionally the one who suggests the need.

Incidentally, there's one vital element in arranging annual reviews that I've inadvertently neglected to mention: My secretaries call each client as a reminder of the annual review appointment. If it's a morning session, the call is placed on the preceding day. For Monday morning appointments, confirmations are made on the preceding Friday. Incidentally, Mondays generally account for the most no-shows of any day of the week, probably because of the weekend interval between phone call and appointment day. Regardless, my secretaries tell me that without this timely reminder, an estimated one-third of my appointments would fail to materialize at the designated date and hour.

I employ a variation on annual reviews for the approximately 40 major accounts among my clientele. Starting in December, calls to the majors are made to establish appointments in January and February, allowing roughly three weeks from the day of the call for the get-together.

Now, if I've been such a certified sales leader, why doesn't everybody—at least in my own office—conduct annual client reviews? In fact, only approximately five out of our 45–50 force do so as a matter of course. My colleagues certainly know what I've accomplished year after year. They've heard me maintain repeatedly that these in-my-office reviews triple my contacts and productivity and that they could at least *double* theirs if they followed suit.

The answers (excuses) I get are strictly in the realm of mythology—and where I part company. For example, I'm satisfied most physicians did not abandon house calls because of greed or insensitivity. Instead, their patient load and need for availability to an ever-increasing and more demanding population drove them to it.

My situation, and that of similar occupations, is different only to a degree. I wanted increased volume despite the fact that people were not knocking down the door to get to me. And I am totally convinced that most of my clients not only appreciate annual reviews but are pleased to come to my office for such sessions. That goes particularly for high-level executives. They appreciate getting away from their own business environment to concentrate without distractions on their own and their families' financial well-being. The same goes for the less affluent. They tell me they'd rather come to my office, or have me take them to breakfast or lunch, than sit around a table at home. Conversely, I'm delighted to be able to dispense with the nonproductive chit-chat that inevitably occurs with a home visit.

Sure, I'll devote a little time to socializing; that's only being courteous. But there's a business-oriented aura that goes with going to a business setting that focuses on one of the most important concerns in anyone's life—his or her financial portfolio. The salesperson who thinks he's imposing on a client by inviting her to his office, or that he's compromising the client's comfort level and is thereby potentially jeopardizing the relationship, is operating under a very false impression.

This is not to say I never encounter resistance to an in-office client review. When I do, I simply adjust to the situation. But those are rare exceptions.

It's a theme I've been stressing in my role as teacher/speaker at every educational level and course I conduct, literally all around the globe. And I'm encouraged that that message is starting to sink in, especially among the younger agents. They are more inclined to have a heartening give-it-a-try attitude, which usually is followed by the pleasant glow of discovery that old John isn't just forever blowing bubbles. Gradually, they're ratcheting up the percentage of both annual reviews and in-office or breakfast/luncheon conferences. The earlier the start, the easier the transition. Once that direction is taken, I maintain that the effective, service-driven salesperson will never revert to time-consuming, minimally productive house calls. You have an office; why not *use* it?

Obviously, I'm not referring to a retail sales clerk or someone hawking hot dogs at the ball park. But I *am* including a vast array of salespeople who can and should profit from annual customer reviews, the majority of whom do not have face-to-face contacts with the folks who put the bread on their tables.

Take car sales. Admittedly, most of us do not buy a new car every year. However, many people purchase one every other year. And a whole lot more hit the buying mode after the third year. Yet rare is the car seller who approaches his customer until year four. A perfect opportunity—for the competition. If I were selling automobiles, I'd be face-to-facing it *annually* with each of my customers. Nothing prolonged; nothing complex. Just meeting, pressing the flesh, showing concern about how the customer's being treated by the service department, etc. Breakfast or lunch, your place or mine; whatever is most convenient. You see, I would want to extend a favorable relationship, or discover what might possibly be jeopardizing it, and find a solution—because I would not only want to survive as a car salesman but also thrive, and because, for car sales and countless other products and services, times aren't changing, they've changed!

THE IMPACT OF GLOBAL COMPETITION

We're light years from the 1960s and 1970s. The United States was top dog, spending huge amounts for guns (Vietnam) and butter (every fad imaginable). It was made to order for order-takers. Selling was a relative cinch. But Japan has already eaten a giant's share off our plate (cars, TVs, recorders). The rest of Asia has been gobbling up what had been our firm grip on clothes (check the labels reading China, Taiwan, Korea). Germany's been phenomenal. And coming through the tunnel like the mother of all freight trains is a financially unified Europe. Somewhere behind is what could pan out to be a market-driven collection of former Soviet states. Free trade among the United States, Canada and Mexico holds staggering potential. Even massive China is tinkering ever so gingerly with the profit motive. Yep, times have changed; and by the year 2000, today's changes will look penny-ante.

Our corporations/businesses have been wising up to those stark realities. They're beginning to realize that their old buyers who aren't shrewd enough to buy effectively are as big a liability as the static salesmen who still think they can finesse a deal with martini-laced lunches and golf sessions that dissipate their afternoons. Enter parades of consultants, psychologists, behavioral scientists, training specialists—supposedly to reshape a sales force resistant to change and, often as not, taught by people who really don't have a clue as to what selling is all about. They grope to make silk purses out of sows' ears, struggling to reshape mediocrities whose measure of success boils down to a forlorn shrug and the assertion that they're "doing OK."

Merely "doing OK" won't survive the reality of the United States being confronted with an ever-diminishing slice of the business pie. The options are crystal clear: We either recruit brighter, better-educated, product-knowledgeable, *people-oriented* salespeople (matched with highly motivated service personnel) who are led by service-smart sales pros, or we lose our shirts, pants, socks, the works. Think it can't happen, that I'm overreacting? Tell that to an auto industry that only a few decades ago had the world as its oyster. Or tell it to the hundreds of thousands of auto assembly-line workers who've been pink-slipped, with many more to follow.

We can't pass along a better society to our kids if we are second-best in our workplace. It follows that we've got to not only satisfy our present customers but keep looking for new ones. That formula does not jibe with the company that relies on 50 to 90 percent of its business from a single customer. One key death, or a corporate demise, and you may as well break out the pallbearers. Sadly, we're not in shape nationally to cut loose the sales forces capable of prospecting for the new customers that can replace the King Kongs.

The sales race isn't won by the swift but by the sure. It's won by cultivating prospects who have a limited amount of disposable income and a desire to be served satisfactorily on every level, and who are increasingly susceptible to growing legions of competitors with the same consideration in mind—their bottom lines.

P. T. Barnum may have underestimated our population growth when he calculated that a sucker was born every minute. Sure, there are suckers. There are also more sophisticated shoppers—people who take seriously the old admonition "buyer beware." They are questioning, skeptical, cautious. Fool them once, shame on you; fool them twice, they figure, it's shame on them. Being underserved or ignored is, to them, the equivalent of being fooled.

To avoid making such a fatal impression, and contrary to that old slogan "work smarter, not harder," we have to do both—work smarter and work harder. Ignite a spark in the customer's eyes and keep it there.

It won't happen by picking up on another dated buzzword, marketing. For now and into the foreseeable future, the only buzzwords that will count are sales, sales and sales. As a nation, that involves using more smarts than we've ever collectively possessed. And it involves working harder at it than we've ever worked. We've missed one train and have paid an exorbitant price to our international competitors. The only other train we'll ever see in our lifetime is now at the station. Truly, we cannot afford to miss it.

7

Selling in the Insurance Business

Often, after speaking before an insurance sales group, I've heard either "Gee, I just can't sell like you," or "Man, I envy the way you express yourself."

I suppose those were meant to be compliments; however, one John F. Savage is enough! More to the point, envy is ignorance, and imitation is suicide. I'm not out to make clones who'll function exactly as I function in selling. Retain your uniqueness, including your capacity for self-expression. Fluency comes with practice and experience. Be yourself. I'll give you plenty of specifics and how I handle them. But the details are meant to form some useful, adaptable *outlines*—not a prescription for lock-step replication. Each of us is different. I would neither expect nor want you to copy everything I do. My purpose will have been served if you garner some useful, adaptable insights that simplify your method of operation and make you more productive.

One of the most important factors in selling is the planning phase—the original thought process of how to acquire a new client. Hence, this chapter will explain how I do it. The ever-present objective: to sell to everyone who is referred to me (I propose sales strictly according to referrals). Operating by way of referrals was something I learned after devoting a long time to getting started. Fortunately, I'm able to help a great number of young people get up to speed much faster and much better than the trial-and-error pattern I groaned through.

HOW TO CULTIVATE REFERRALS

My client list numbers roughly 900. Of that total, I rely on approximately 30 as references to prospective customers. Obviously, those who enable my access to others are themselves very satisfied clients and hold influential positions—e.g., a top executive to whom colleagues pay attention. I keep in frequent touch with these valuable resources. They are the conduits to my sales growth.

The scenario for making a new connection varies. More often than not, a prime client will casually mention my name to a colleague in a conversation, along the lines of "John Savage helped me on such-and-such a problem. I think you'd do yourself a favor by just talking with him for a little bit. See what he may have to offer you." No big deal. Nothing about pressure. It's simply one person planting a seed that could be beneficial to two others—the acquaintance and me. This kind of referral is more likely immediately after I've performed an especially appreciated service. It's a subtle phenomenon. People just naturally like doing things for someone who's been helpful to them and in whom they have confidence.

The other approach is to ask a client to mention me to a person he or she knows and who I believe is a potentially sound prospect. Either way, once I get the nod to make a contact, I'll call to confirm that everything is agreeable and set up an appointment—breakfast, lunch, my office, whatever is most convenient.

PUTTING THE CLIENT AT EASE

At the first get-together, I have programmed my thinking toward two inflexible rules: to be a good listener and never press for a sale. Being pushy was never in vogue; in today's business world, pushiness is certain death to any hopes for a lasting client.

Another guideline: Make that first meeting as comfortable for your guest as you possibly can (which is where listening instead of talking is such an asset). Eventually, the prospect will get around to asking, "John, just what *is* it that you do?" My answer: I help people manage their money, which includes making them aware that the greatest economic disease in the country is spending.

That latter phrase is an uncommon grabber. It sets up a little story I've been using lately to further an underlying theme. It starts off with the observation that the buying public has the funny notion that they save money by pumping their own gas at a service station. The client comments, "Well, people *do* save money by pumping their own gas." I respond: When the customer finishes pumping the gas, do they come out to get his money, or does he go in to pay? Answer: "Of course, he goes in to pay." Me: But that self-pumper has walked into a trap—the food trap: M&Ms, pop, peanuts, cookies, etc. If, as is most often the case, the customer is gassing up on his way home from work, he's also more inclined to cut the edge off his appetite with one or more of the tempting morsels he encounters when he goes in to pay his bill. If he buys one modest snack (convincing himself it won't spoil his meal), he'll probably come out even for having pumped his gas. If he buys anything else, his gas will cost more than if he'd gone to a full-service operation. The gas station operator has made a sizable investment, betting that the customer *will not* end up saving money. It's want vs. need, with want usually winning the contest. It's the reason you see so many service stations remodel so that the number of pumps remains the same, but the area for food, drinks, toys, etc., is expanded.

The gas pump on the outside has grown a grocery/knick-knack store on the inside to make more money from the person who pumps his own gas—and who thinks he's saving some money by doing so.

STRESS THE IMPORTANCE OF SAVING

The purpose behind that little yarn (or one similar to it) is to get the prospect into an interested mood to discuss saving. It's an effective tool, tied as it is to my follow-up: i.e., societal pressures make it increasingly difficult to save. In other words, I'm sympathizing with the great majority (probably including the prospect) who are constantly inundated with advertising, telephone solicitations ("You've just won one of four fabulous prizes!"), point-of-purchase displays and other clever devices to separate people from their incomes. However, I go on to say, *most of my clients are good savers,* because we meet at least once a year for savings reviews and related services I can provide them—a regular check-up. In that, I'm injecting a crucial facet of the selling process that has declined rapidly in the past 20 years. We all know what it's like to go to a department store and discover it's easier to find a product than it is to root out a clerk, or to promote pleasantries at a busy restaurant, only to have the waiter come back with the wrong order or the food cold. Signs of the times, even during a recession. But it is this very pronounced lack of service that can distinguish the salesperson who does serve, who thinks continuously of innovative ways to serve clients and who builds a base on the strong referrals of satisfied customers.

After establishing a comfortable setting, when I'm satisfied we've "baked a cake," I invite the prospect to come to my office (as opposed to my earlier years, when I went to the client's office). If it's a business client, he or she usually comes alone. If it's a family client, the spouses generally show up as a team. For purposes of this example, I'll use a session with husband and wife.

THE FAMILY SESSION

When they arrive at the appointed hour, I seat them at a round table for four, the spouses side by side. I'm seated with them, with a "whiteboard" directly behind me. After the greetings are exchanged and we're all at ease, I stand up in front of the board, facing my visitors. If you've read or heard how I conduct such meetings, you know how heavily I employ that board in outlining and reinforcing what I have to relate. Standing before them, instead of being seated with them, is plain psychology, rooted in the teacher/student relationship—and I'm the teacher. I'm fully convinced that this standing/sitting arrangement offers maximum advantage to the sales agent. From years of experience, I've learned that such positioning supports the fact that people are really willing to listen if they think you care about them and can offer something of benefit.

The Financial Analysis

So here's the family composition: The husband is age 45, his wife 43 years old. Both are college graduates. Their three children are ages 18, 16 and 13. Once I get the age spread on the kids, I know there's a likely concern about putting them through college. I uncover that their annual income is $60,000, all via the father; mother stays at home. I suspect, without asking at this point, that they don't have over $10,000 in the bank (an informed hunch, gleaned from decades of interviews that revealed an incredible absence of savings). Most of their money is probably tied up in his 401(k) plan at work, pension, profit sharing, and maybe even an IRA that was put together 15 years ago and that hasn't had a new deposit added to it in the last 12 years. Today it's worth perhaps $15,000. These are presumptions—but you have to have some presumptions derived from the first informal meeting before you can start developing a financial management program. You'll retain the ability to adjust as precise circumstances dictate. The specifics soon materialize . . . and I'm rarely surprised.

The details emerge as I start scribbling the Family Finance Tree (see Figure 7.1) on my whiteboard, always with the same three circles denoting "bank," "investments" and "insurance," and always with the same stated priority: the bank account. That's an all-important concession. Put that "bank account" in your top priority drawer and lock it in, because almost nobody says this (except a banker). You see, the banker promotes banking, the broker promotes investments and the insurance practitioner talks about insurance. If you get nothing more out of this book, let is be *not* to be like everybody else. Your job, in the predictable future of financial planning/money management, is to discuss all three elements—banking, investing, insuring—in an intelligent manner. People want to avoid having to deal with a representative for each of those elements. They want to feel comfortable with one overall adviser.

Figure 7.1 Family Finance Tree

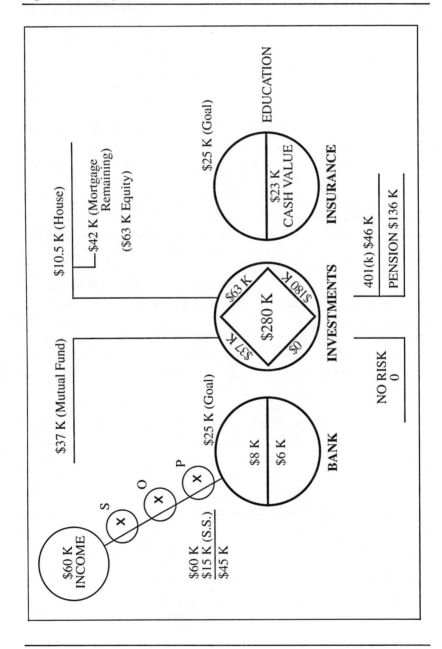

So when I tell prospects that a bank account is the most important thing in financial planning, and certainly the most important savings vehicle, I have set myself apart from other insurance agents—especially when I make it abundantly clear that I make my living *solely* from the sale of life insurance. However, I also ram that point home with this point: I feel I have a responsibility, based on years of accumulating pertinent data, to help my clients in *every* area of personal financial management.

Next, I fire this potent zinger to my husband/wife audience: "You probably don't have any idea how many people there are, just like yourselves, who do not have $25,000 in the bank." Invariably, their response is, "Why, we don't have $25,000 in the bank." I ask how much they do have in the bank. "$6,000." Then quickly: "Would you *like* to have $25,000 in the bank?" Answer from almost everyone in a similar spot: "Certainly!"

But rather than camp there, I move to the middle circle on the board (investments) and say, "Then you must understand that, if you're going to make strides in our capitalistic system, ultimately 90 percent of your money has to be in investments." Here's where you demonstrate that you're firmly on the side of the prospect. Let's see now what the interview has thus far revealed: The family has $6,000 banked; the net worth of their house, the money in their pension/profit-sharing/401(k) and a couple of mutual funds they purchased total $280,000 in the middle circle. Obviously, they already have more than 90 percent of their money in the investments circle, for which I compliment them.

Then—and if only I could get this inside the head of every insurance salesperson—I lay this one on the duo: "Insurance is the *least* important part of financial planning." Why this apparent downgrading of insurance? Reality, friend. Insurance in this context is truly least important in the mind of the buyer. Conduct a poll. Ask people if they'd rather have their money in a bank or in insurance. Brace yourself for the answers. Try finding one in 50 favoring insurance. Then try again. Prospects must be educated as to the *relative* importance of insurance. Me, I'm obviously sold on the value of insurance; I have a $3 million policy on my life. Buy, hey, I'm *in* insurance. If clothing were my game, I'd probably have a much larger closet full of suits.

Back to where we left off during the interview, I ask to look at the insurance policies the couple brought for my examination. (I always ask them to bring in any documents concerning their finances: will, policies, the works). I do not prescribe to the timeworn, time-wasting process of gathering a prospect's policies, carting them back to the office to evaluate them and set up a "program," then returning with a fancily printed recommendation. What a dissipation of time—and what a farce! Anyone short of brain-dead ought to be able to evaluate an insurance policy in 20 *seconds*. It only has three meaningful pages: the cover, showing the amount; the cash value; and the application that the client has signed. The rest is filler as far as the prospect goes. The filler may be necessary from a legal standpoint, and to satisfy the needs of a home office or even those of a practitioner. But buyers seldom ever open a policy. To them, it's a yawner.

Presenting the Plan

So, with the prospects' documents reviewed by me in their presence, I've used up all of two minutes to determine that they have $200,000 worth of life insurance and a cumulative cash value of $23,000, which goes into the right (insurance) circle. This meshes with $6,000 in the first (bank) circle and the $280,000 in the middle (investments) circle, where they have over 90 percent of their financial pie. I'm able to tell them that, with the latter element, they're well on their way toward their retirement and security nest-egg. I applaud them on the admirable balance of their package. I embellish that applause by letting them know that the $23,000 cash value of their life insurance can be used as a down payment for a college education. For a traditional policy, I explain that they can borrow money out of the contracts. If the policy is universal life, they can reduce the amount of the death benefit by the amount taken. Pleasant surprise registers on their faces (as often happens during such interviews). They allow as that's really nice to know, because they'd been wondering where they'd find the money for that all-important purpose. This leads me nicely into an in-depth discussion of college education, the while trying to minimize their fears as to how they'll be able to bankroll their kids' higher learning. I tell them I've found, with my seven boys, that it's not difficult for them to earn the money to pay for half of the education bill. With girls it's a harder chore, because they have less access to good-paying jobs at that age. But in any event, I tell them truthfully that most of my clients manage to survive the sticker shock of seeing their children through to a college diploma by way of savings, loans, grants, scholarships and a whole array of resources that I keep up-to-date on and that I'm happy to share with them.

You don't have to be the parent of a large, college-age brood to acquire this information. A young, single insurance agent can become well versed in it just as easily—and be prepared to offer advice of great interest to many of his clients/prospects. This has nothing to do with direct selling of insurance; but it has a whale of a lot to do with providing the unexpected, "different" service that can make an insurance agent invaluable to his clientele.

From there we move into what historically has been taught as "programming." As I learned it in the Life Underwriters Training Council, one was supposed to get a lot of information, evaluate it and come back with a life insurance proposal, as integrated with Social Security, to effect total family security if premature death should occur. Well, I've been able to reduce this process to its simplest equation. Namely, if your income is, say, $60,000 a year, you should be able to leave $60,000 a year. That $60K income I write in a circle on the upper-left corner of the board. I explain that Social Security will contribute $15,000 a year, which is subtracted from the $60,000, leaving a balance/need of $45,000 per year, without depleting principal. Now, I say that $700,000 will be needed, the income from which will provide that net $45,000 annually. The prospect/family already has $300,000. Of the remaining goal of $400,000, they already have $200,000 in face value life insurance, leaving the same dollar amount yet to get. Which, I advise them, they can achieve with a premium payment of $40 or $50 a month, depending on the company and the specific policy they buy. They are delighted. A solid relationship has been formed.

Postscript: Until last year, I had dictated a detailed write-up on every such interview, filing it for the annual review. It took a lot of my time to dictate and chewed up 20 hours per week of typing by one of my two secretaries. Then, unlike trying to teach an old dog new tricks, I suddenly remembered a fascinating exercise in summarizing I'd first encountered in a study hall as a high school freshman! Talk about never being too old to relearn. The teacher monitoring the study room showed us how, if we were listening to the radio at home, we could program an entire football game on one sheet of paper. What he did was to impress upon us the inconsequential downtime in any such contest—timeouts, players walking away from huddles, penalties, etc.—and how few actual plays occurred during the two hours of the game. With that far-removed lesson as inspiration, I designed a seven-line summation of a client interview. How much is in the bank, cash value of life insurance, investments, what's in the four corners of the investments—that's it. So when the secretary comes in after the client leaves, she takes only the information needed to type those seven lines. It's over and done with in a few minutes. It's lopped off hours from my back and from my secretary's—time which can be used for much more productive purposes, to say nothing of gaining relief from nonessential tedium.

Moral: We don't have to do what's historically been done. Indeed, we must be very different about numerous key phases of our operation, such as during the interview and where it takes place. We must service the account on no less than an annual basis. And, when we've cultivated the right kind of client relationships, we can mail the policies and other pertinent data to them; it isn't necessary to hand-deliver. Think—about conserving your and your staff's time, about using referrals, about rehearsing an interview, about putting an insurance sale into the client's perspective, about advising far beyond the limited parameters of insurance—and you stand to double your productivity consistently.

CUSTOMIZED SERVICE PAYS
LONG-TERM DIVIDENDS

You've got to put yourself in their shoes—and this is where I think many a life insurance practitioner fails. Too often agents wade in with a predetermined insurance contract (and preordained premium) that the "prospect should have." Ignored are the needs of and demands on the individuals they're trying to sell. Recognizing this factor takes a little time and a lot of understanding, and perhaps a pinch of wisdom. But hear this: It works. Unless you're ready to individualize each presentation with the need of the individual considered, you're not going to be effective. And you will be working just as hard at age 60 as you were at age 35.

Again, the game has changed. There are many more people than when I started 40-odd years ago who are trying to capture the citizenry's dollars. TV has eroded much of its conventional programming to make room for half-hour commercials. Regular programs are bloated with ads. There's a magazine now for virtually every interest. It's been authoritatively estimated that the average consumer is bombarded by 5,000 commercial messages *a day*—newspapers, radio, TV, handbills, billboards, matchbooks, junk mail, phone calls—an endless cacophony of pitches. If you take the time to personally involve yourself with each prospective buyer, there's no question in my mind you'll build a steady, appreciative clientele—one that can see, meet and touch you. This will put you among the top ten of those with whom they do business.

Know it: There's less genuinely personal service now than ever—and there are more people than ever not getting any. Show them kindness and understanding, spend time, service their account—and they won't do business with anyone else. Service has gone from good to fair to poor to none. Really serve and you'll discover you have very little competition in the field.

8

Effective Office Procedures

FURNISHINGS AND DECOR

Organize your office for its sole purpose: to conduct business. Equip and furnish it with that exclusive purpose in mind. Keep it bare-bones simple and plain comfortable, emphasis on the plain. Keep away from furniture and exhibits that collectively smack of ostentation. Clients and prospects really aren't interested in the ego trips and blatant self-promotion of anyone whose object is to serve *them*. A wall full of plaques on how great you are might stroke your self-image but may just as readily transmit a negative nonverbal message—"this guy's stuck on himself." A fancy $5,000 desk is not likely to gain points with the client who not only cannot afford such a luxury but whose own "desk" is nothing other than a kitchen table, with a ceiling light for illumination. Avoid any implication that you are either egotistical or too expensive for even the little guy's pocketbook. Never forget: That little guy is very important as is; and you can never know whether he'll make it to the big leagues and will want to keep you along for the ride.

Of course, I'm not suggesting you should go to the opposite extreme—antiseptic walls, furniture that looks like it came from a third-rate garage sale, an air of sterile cheerlessness. You can have a highly effective office atmosphere without resorting to a shred of pretension. Whatever image you portray, ask yourself whether it is tasteful without being glitzy and whether it actually serves a purpose.

In my own shop, I have a credenza whose main function is to hold my telephones within convenient reach, off my desk. The desk itself is average size, modest and utilitarian. My clients and I do our talking at a nearby round table, with four chairs. I have a couch to accommodate a few more visitors on the rare occasions when a contingency arises. I have yet to take a nap on that couch. If I feel the need to lie down, I go home and go to bed. Offices are for working.

In proximity to the table and chairs, I have a "whiteboard." I use it to illustrate what I'm discussing with the client, in much the same way a coach writes Xs and Os to illustrate what he's been verbalizing. It's an extremely valuable tool. It helps clarify the critical points I'm trying to convey. Equally important, it implants in the client-observer's mind images that are simple and easy to recall.

Carpeting? Yes, my office is carpeted—at least it was the last time I noticed, which is I don't know when. It hasn't been a high-priority concern. As a matter of fact, when I had to be away from the office for an extended spell, my two secretaries had the carpeting replaced, on the reasonable grounds that the original had been, in their valued judgment, worn to shreds. Two weeks after the new installation, the ladies asked for my reaction. If it had been a snake, it would've bitten me. I hadn't even noticed the redo.

Aim for Comfort and Efficiency

The same goes for square footage. As long as I can function efficiency and effectively, and as long as I'm convinced my clients are comfortable in my office, I don't have much concern about office acreage. I don't want vast, open spaces with a clear-day-you-can-see-forever view. Three years ago, my secretaries told me they needed more space. What those ladies need, they *need*. My quick response? Lop off some of my office. They got the room I did not require. Everybody's happy. Maintaining happiness—particularly where the staff numbers up to 50 agents and 30 or so secretaries—is a constant pursuit. Unhappy people cannot be productive for long. Furthermore, I feel that, while I cannot expect to provide an atmosphere where close associates are continually in a state of glee, I do have a moral imperative to do all I possibly can to eliminate stress and to maximize genuine cooperativeness and office esprit. Also, feeling better at work can do a lot to mitigate external pressures which everyone encounters at home, with friends and relatives, etc. It doesn't take anything more than keeping your eyes and ears open, and then exercising some empathy and consideration for your fellow human beings.

However, I also want myself and my secretaries sequestered from the hubbub of the rest of the operation. I don't mean to put us in a vacuum, devoid of any chance of associate interfacing. I do mean to reduce the opportunity for idle visiting that can throw efficiency to the four winds. The key at work is to keep one's eye on the rabbit. Distractions corrode the key. That's why my office is adjacent to my secretaries', the door between is open, and our combined space is somewhat removed from the remainder of the floor on which we function. I'm not constitutionally inclined to be the proverbial taskmaster, constantly goading subordinates. I seek out and get good people who have the right attitude, aptitude and sense of responsibility to get the job done, every day. I let them do their job. And my ladies work!

My work room does contain a few personal items: one plaque denoting membership in the million-dollar roundtable (there could be dozens, which would indicate either megalomania or rampant self-doubt); a crucifix, as a reminder of what my existence is all about—and that I've never quite measured up; a map from wife, Kate, with red dots indicating where I've speechified/lectured (nobody else knows what the dots represent, unless I'm asked); a picture of my family—and that's about it. Granted, a crucifix is not a commonplace in an office setting. But to me, it symbolizes the most influential thing in my life; the source of my existence; the bedrock if my family; the embodiment of love and hope. I want that representation of Christ everywhere I go—home, office, car, around my neck. Because when I get down to *that,* nothing else in life really matters.

SUPPORT STAFF

Aside from your personal input, no one's is more critical to your office than that of your secretary, or, in my case, secretaries. I consider mine irreplaceable. Their prescribed schedule runs from 8:30 a.m. to 5 p.m., with an hour off for lunch. They are anything but clock-watchers. They invariably work beyond the normal quitting time. Exceptional? Certainly! They stand in sharp contrast to the legions who are primed to jump ship a half-hour or more before the bell. They're a happy "crew" that makes for a happy "ship." As the "captain," I tell them I can dictate their environment, but I can't direct the sea. What I mean is that I'll try to make their working conditions as pleasant for them as I possibly can, that I'll give them a free rein to do their respective things, but that there are forces beyond our control which will occasionally but inevitably rock our boat. Nevertheless, we have to strive against having a bad day. We cannot control the action of a client; we can control our reaction— i.e., always be receptive, accommodating, pleasant.

I have two secretarial gems. But I didn't find them falling from a tree or by way of a headhunter. When I'm in the hiring mode, I engage in a strenuous search. This does not entail examining résumés. I refuse to look at them. For the most part, they are inherently fraudulent. In the days when I did bother to scan résumés as a courtesy for others, I noted that none ever acknowledged that the applicant wound up in the lower one-third of his or her graduating class. By implication, just about everyone is in the upper third. It's among the reasons I recommended in a speech recently at the University of Nevada/Las Vegas that job-seekers forgo writing a résumé (unless arbitrarily prescribed by the prospective employer).

Because everybody does it, they're invitations to exaggeration and they're often intellectually dishonest. Even if they were as accurate as the written word can convey, résumés are immaterial to my searches. You see, when it comes to a secretary, I'm not looking for a stenographer, or a filing clerk, or someone who's quick on dictation or can type like a machine gun. I'm looking for what I cannot discover in a résumé, no matter how long or expansive it may be. I'm looking for "bright." And I can't find "bright" via paper—résumé, test or any related screening process.

It takes going head-to-head, talking. In less than an hour, I can find out whether the interviewee is not only industrious but has "it": the understanding that the most important thing pertaining to my operation is the client. Those are pretty much givens nowadays. But they're meaningless for me if they don't also include that all-essential characteristic of making the client the focal point of every job-related chore they undertake.

My senior secretary, Wilma Glaser, has been with me 13 years. She was trained by the wonderful lady who worked for me the preceding 17 years. Wilma had impressive credentials. I met her when I was chairman of the board at the University of Toledo and she, with a background in English, was secretary to the university's president. But while it was obvious that she was a splendid secretary for a top school administrator, it wasn't until I had a face-to-face session that I was satisfied Wilma could meet my expectations. She's done so every day since she's signed on. I wanted, needed and got a great secretary. You should settle for no less in your operation.

I did comparably well in hiring my second secretary, Lisa Heinrich. Lisa is one of a number of local high school students our agency hires temporarily when they're 16 years old, to give them some secretarial experience as well as to allow us to observe the best young ladies among a very good crop. Not a Diane Dimbulb in the lot. Then, when they're age 19 and have their diplomas, we're in an excellent position, if there's a job opening, to offer full-time employment to the créme de la créme. It's as big a benefit for us as it is for the young lady hired. It's the route Lisa took in joining our organization. The choice was right on the mark: Lisa and Wilma have worked harmoniously and very effectively for the past nine years. I place enormous confidence in them, and they know it. I've told them often enough that if they left at this stage in my life, we'd *all* go. Sad, isn't it, that so many commendable people can work for an organization, get straight "A" evaluations for years—then be dumped on the slag heap via corporate cutbacks.

Offer Compensation That Counts

Along with "empowering" Wilma and Lisa and complimenting them
on their work, I also compensate them very well. Kind words are
important and, when sincerely delivered, much appreciated. But words
alone don't pay anybody's bills. If I have a shortcoming in this inter-
relationship, it's in never being able to remember when Secretaries'
Week falls. When that forgetfulness manifests itself every year—as
habitually as fleas zero in on a hound dog—I ask the ladies if they'd
rather be recognized on Secretaries' Day or on the two days each year
(May and Christmas) when I give them their bonuses, over and above
a very good paycheck throughout the year. Funny, but the bonuses win
out every time.

I don't take my secretaries to lunch—period. We don't have
"attitude adjustment hours." Two reasons: I don't think secretary-em-
ployer luncheons or similar social tete-a-tetes constitute a good mix.
And my lunch times are usually slotted for meetings with a client or
prospect, as are my breakfasts. Briefly, I work throughout the day—and
love it. Working breakfast, office, working lunch, office; dinner at
home; then, frequently, some "homework," such as working on a book
or giving a speech. I give about 40 speeches a year, half domestic, half
out of town. In addition, many of my trips around the world are
combinations of pleasure and career-related speeches and consulta-
tions. Kate usually accompanies me (thank God), and we have a great
time. But I also know when it's time to get away from the workday
routine and recharge the batteries. Generally, that's during the summer,
when I'll cut loose for two or three months at a crack—and still wind
up outselling everyone else in our company and just about anywhere
else, for that matter.

To repeat myself, great secretaries are pivotal to my pace and
performance. Ergo, when they need a gadget, piece of equipment or
whatever, I let *them* go pick it out. Too liberal? Too patronizing? Not
if they're superb secretaries. I don't know anything about gadgets. I
know a lot about how I want to produce. They know that and will ask
for or acquire equipment to fulfill that purpose. And I don't get hung
up on the costs involved; I know they'll be prudent, in the final analysis.
For example, my whiteboard needed to be replaced after 15 years of

wear and tear. Just like with that worn-out office carpet I mentioned previously, I hadn't noticed. The ladies took care of it. I couldn't have cared less about the price. You see, this was a basic tool I'd employed in negotiating literally hundreds of millions of dollars worth of policies. I'm not about to quibble about relative cost to get a new and better product. I trust, absolutely, my secretaries' discretion in obtaining what I *need*.

So, if you're in a comparable service-oriented position, you'd better make certain you have extraordinary secretarial assistance.

USING TIME WISELY

If you are perceptive and patient enough to seek out such unique help, you'll readily avoid wasting mind-boggling amounts of time—time you should be devoting to your clients and prospects. Please, do me a favor by pledging that you'll never open your mail—or, heaven forbid, go to get it at the post office or wait at the door for the mailman. A squirrel or beaver can open mail! A solid secretary can protect you against 90 percent of your correspondence, as well as 90 percent of your telephone calls! I never look at an advertisement; Lisa lobs them right into the wastebasket, where they won't bother me. Only roughly 10 percent of my mail and calls require my attention, things my secretaries cannot handle on their own. Essentially, that 10 percent pertains to people who are hurting or who may be unhappy with some aspect of my operation—who really warrant my attention on that score. These include primarily widows, several widowers and retirees who seek direction on their annuities, insurance or disability income. Those calls and letters, my secretaries understand, are a number one priority. Whenever appropriate, even if I'm overseas, I'll return calls, or the secretaries will arrange to have the client call me collect when the latter approach would be the most expeditious.

They also understand that they are never to tell a caller who needs to speak with me that "John's not in" when, in fact, I am. If I'm unavailable at the moment, they take the message and respond that I'll be back to them as soon as I can—and I do just that. I can follow this super-efficient office procedure because my secretaries have such a beautiful relationship with my clients. They're not only sincerely courteous, caring and attentive, they also have the knowledge and experience to resolve, right then and there, the vast majority of client inquiries they field.

I believe in accessibility, always, to my clients and elimination of *everything* I can delegate effectively to my helpers. Over the years—and the last ten have been my most productive—this delegation has resulted in the conservation of thousands of hours which I can devote to my clients, at least 50 of whom I meet with 10 to 20 times a year. I use those precious hours to concentrate on the enormous challenge of meeting client financial needs. The proof that my method does work, to a record-setting degree, is there for the seeing; not brag, pure fact. I just want to see the message spread—and tried. Bottom line: It will make for many more successful salespeople who, as a result, will have a far more satisfying life for themselves and for everyone else within their reach.

9

The Big Client

While each client is important, most of us in sales segregate customers into three general categories: big (from large to gigantic), midsize and small. Each is an important part of your total portfolio. You must dedicate yourself to serving the "little guy" as well as the bigger and biggest ones. First, there's the basic responsibility to look after your contacts' best interests. Second, never lose sight of the fundamental advisability of diversifying your clientele—of never putting too few eggs in your basket. And third, there's that previously stated phenomenon of seeing that "little guy" blossom into the jumbo ranks. It happens with dizzying regularity.

However, this portion of my book is devoted to the extraordinary client—large in terms of sheer size and influence. It is written for the mature, experienced professional who has worked long and hard at prospecting, developing and selling. It involves a quest which, in my experience, typically takes a lot of time—easily two or three years of very patient, unobtrusive communication with prospects who are involved with demanding, intricate operations and who are inherently cautious in their decision making. You have to respect that wariness. They have an awful lot on their minds. They are often painfully aware that whatever they decide, many others' welfare—jobs, financial future, family—depends on their objectivity and clearheadedness, and on their degree of precaution.

I've got to add this: Beyond the complex challenge of prospecting for big clients, I've also had the tremendous good fortune of encountering and becoming a close friend of some of the finest people God ever put into shoe leather. Looking back after having made it as a very successful salesman, I can relish the fact that these friendships, mixed with those from the small and midsize transactions, have been essential ingredients to a full and happy life.

While I indicated that this segment was geared toward seasoned professional salespeople who are in the best position to prospect for the big client, I don't overlook the less experienced or the beginner. Anybody can learn from the experiences of another. Also, the new kid on the block can beat formidable odds by landing a biggie right out of the blue. But that kind of luck is usually consigned to miracles and lottery winners. Winning the lottery is a fluke, a one in a million-plus shot. You cannot build a pattern out of that brand of sand castle. On the other hand, you can gain access to a prize prospect by way of youthful friendship and/or through a relative's friendship. But getting even a good acquaintance to lend you an ear is no guarantee of landing a deal.

PATIENCE PAYS OFF

Take my first big client, my first big break. I was 24 years of age at the time, long on guts and short on brains. I paid a call on Jim Gerity, a prominent Michigan broadcaster whose father and mine were the closest of friends. Jim was roughly twice my age—and easily 100 times as smart. I can't recall exactly how I broached the subject, but the words somehow stumbled out that my purpose was to talk with him about insurance. I recall Jim's response in a nutshell: If, five years down the road, I was still in the insurance business, come back and see him and we'd have that talk. I thanked him, said goodbye and bided my time. Five years later, while I was paying a courtesy visit to Jim's elderly dad, Jim poked his head in the room, learned I was still in the insurance business and invited me to come and see him in a week. When I appeared as directed, Jim called in an associate, Al Wolflee, and informed him, "I want John to take over our group insurance." You could've knocked me over with the proverbial feather. Here I was, age

29, just married, beating out what I was to learn were 20 other agencies competing for this contract. I'll never forget: It brought me $3,800 in commissions the first year I was admitted to the Million-Dollar Roundtable. A gift, to be sure—yet Jim had established the ground rule. He wanted to see if I could survive five years in a tough game. I did, without ever once bugging him. I was patient, I did not violate his time condition, and in his view I'd picked up some useful experience that would complement his objectives. For a young, struggling salesman, five years can seem like two eternities back to back. But patience is a virtue that cannot be substituted. You have to discipline yourself to work with it, and do so gracefully, without a hint of agitation. You hate to be pestered; so does your prospect.

SCHOOL TIES CAN LAST A LIFETIME

Patience, youthful association and the peculiarity of coming from and having a large family were instrumental in my serving The Andersons, a legend-in-its-time corporation if ever there was one. It is a major agricultural/retail operation well into its third generation. In northwest Ohio, if you're into a charitable drive, significant civic effort or in search of leadership for virtually any worthy cause, knowing heads recognize that you start with The Andersons. In the late 1940s, the founding father, Harold Anderson, had the courage and spirit to rise from a staggering business failure to what became known as "the big pour." With the strong backs and minds of his strapping sons, Harold led the work force that put together a huge grain elevator/storage complex, while maintaining and expanding a now-thriving retail business.

My first contact with the Andersons (the family, as opposed to the enterprise), occurred in high school (1943–1947), when I met Dick Anderson. We were acquaintances, not pals. Two quick recollections: Dick, who ultimately became CEO of the firm, had hands the size of bear paws; he cut loose from school for a year to partake in "the big pour." It wasn't until 20 years later that I started building a personal relationship with members of the Anderson family. As it developed, the cement in this process formed quickest through Dick to his elder brother, John, who became chairman of the board. Putting it as succinctly as I can, John Anderson was the finest man I ever encountered.

Free Counseling Sets the Stage

Deeply religious, John and I hit it off by virtue of our each being the father of a large brood. At a casual, friendly lunch, discussing peripheral topics evolved to John's asking me what I did. Answer: insurance—and then some. It was the "then some" that whetted his appetite (everyone knows that insurance sales are, right?). I told John I had been offering services to clients and prospects which covered a wide range of subjects related to effective business operations and satisfied, motivated employees. I said I'd learned over the years what impedes efficiency, dissipates sales, lowers morale and engenders fear, and how these obstacles could be surmounted. At that point in my career, I had counseled approximately 25 companies.

That first year, I met with John perhaps 30 times, with him probing how I addressed the perils of management effectiveness, leadership, discipline and sales. I refrained from making an insurance sales pitch in my own behalf.

Satisfied that we were on the same philosophical plane, John invited me to address his staff. And what a staff! They were exceptionally qualified people at every level, and head of the class when it came to being customer service–oriented. Yet, because he was deeply concerned over the welfare of his employees—had devoted large sums to literature as well as a legal staff for employee protection on all fronts— John was disbelieving when I estimated that half his people did not even have a will. He took a random sample. Out of ten respondents, eight admitted they had no will in their respective families. John was disappointed, to say the least, but he also recognized an eye-opener.

Over a three-year span, I kept talking to executives and subordinates at The Andersons on every subject on which they wanted input and which I felt comfortable addressing. As per my firm custom, I declined any and all offers of compensation for this service. Throughout those 36 or so months, my consistent response to proffers of consultant fees was an appreciative no-thanks, followed by my standard: My pay is limited to the commission on the sale of insurance (preferably tied to a total financial planning package). Period. And I studiously avoided making a sales pitch.

Well, rolling into Year Four, John told me more insurance was needed for his brothers, his sister and their ever-expanding families. To that date, we're counting up to 50 kids—not too shabby a volume for a salesman in his late thirties; some $2.5 million in life insurance contracts, paid annually by their trusts, and written up within the space of two weeks.

TOP EXECUTIVES NEED SERVICE, TOO

That was just the beginning. A quick follow-up was in the nature of a lecture I gave on good financial planning. From there we went to individual face-to-face conferences with more than 50 employees, top-level executives included. A point or two with regard to the latter: Too many salespeople think executives are almost unapproachable. It may be more challenging, to be sure, but don't be intimidated by that thought. Many executives have limited involvement with people outside their own companies. They're isolated and preoccupied with their corporate responsibilities. But they have needs as critical as anyone else's. If you take time to cultivate contacts, build the confidence that generates referrals and listen carefully to what's bothering or puzzling them, you can hit executive targets in the bull's-eye. But, *don't waste their time. Use simple words and short sentences.* Forget any fancy footwork or high-toned phraseology. Good executives are prudent clock-watchers—not to get away from their work but to get back at it. Dick Anderson signed up with me. Brother Tom also came in the fold with the uncluttered sentence, "John, I'd like a policy like Dick's."

GOOD NEWS TRAVELS FAST

The individual sessions resulting from my talk before 50-plus employees netted in excess of $5 million in life insurance coverage. More have since followed. The spin-offs continue, and so do the commissions. Five years ago I was invited to join another friend to become the only two outside, nonfamily members of The Andersons board. Aside from my sales commissions, board membership marked the only time I've been paid by the firm for other than selling a policy. But if anything, I've received far more from them than they ever have or will from me. As I was a mentor for them, so were they for me. The exposure gave me an unmatched insight into the workings of a major enterprise, allowing me to squirrel away reams of hands-on experiences.

Then there are the people, starting with the lovable, unpretentious John Anderson—the kind of guy who'd call up my wife, ask what's she's cooking for dinner, then tell her he's on his way to join us. In he'd come, just like family, loaded with gentle wisdom, compassion and unflinching hope. Ironically, John was uninsurable; I couldn't insure the very man who, in so many ways, helped me to write a bonanza of policies. I treasured every minute I spent with him, as I have with his remarkable siblings and colleagues. John's relatively recent death left an unfillable void. He taught me so much in what now seems like the blink of an eye.

I've been similarly blessed in getting to know Rene McPherson. A no-nonsense, skip-the-baloney genius, Rene reworked Dana Corporation into a world-class powerhouse as chairman of the board and chief executive. Then, adhering to his own career strategy, he quit when he reached the preordained age of 55 to become dean of the graduate business college at Stanford University.

We met as speakers at the same conference. Similar styles were quickly evident. One, we both disdained the use of notes and spoke off the cuff. Another, Rene insisted on cutting to the quick; he sliced through management layers to get at the source of a problem. No parades of memos, no filtering down through successions of VPs and associates. Man after my own heart. I'll take a head-to-head talk over memos every time. Rene would go out of his way to talk with the troops, especially cleaning ladies. This wasn't showboating or a flimsy exercise in false empathy. Rene wanted to know what made his plants tick. So he went to the folks who punched and wound the clocks.

Through Rene, I learned how a giant company functioned; it was like getting a tailored Ph.D. in international trade. Oddly enough, I'd learned that John Anderson, for all his community prestige, had failed repeatedly to arrange a meeting with Rene McPherson. Because I'd come to know Rene and had given talks before various groups of his employees (and had sold insurance to them), my reaction was to call Rene's secretary and see if we could pop over, right then and there, and visit with him. We got in without any fuss; I can't even remember the purpose behind John's desire for the session. But the moral was pretty obvious. It's lonely at the top of a huge conglomerate because of the enormous and self-imposed pressures; if you're an unknown, it usually requires a referral—a mutual friend to break through the barrier. It's why, for me, referrals are so crucial to my salesmanship. The principle is all-inclusive. It's "who do you know?" as fully as "what do you know?"

As for Rene, I had the pleasure of seeing my recommendation accepted: He was named a board member of The Andersons, joining me as the only other outsider on that body. I figure I served everyone involved: A corporate giant and former head of one of the most prestigious business schools in the world was helping to advise a superb family enterprise. The operative word: *Serve*—serve your clients well, and beyond the execution of an insurance (or any other kind of) sale.

NEIGHBORLINESS CAN LEAD TO BIGGER THINGS

Now comes this entry in my dissertation on cultivating the big client— with a different twist: Ron Langenderfer, who was to become president and chief executive officer of Stateline Steel. We met as back-fence neighbors at our homes on Pilliod Road in Swanton, Ohio, a Toledo suburb, when he was the top salesman and an officer for Parker Steel Company. I'd never sold insurance to a neighbor; never felt comfortable with the notion. And, as I was to learn later, Ron simply did not like insurance salesmen. However, he was somewhat captivated by the sight of my nine kids gardening and weeding on the one-acre plot behind our house. Where was I on those hot afternoons? Acting as any sensible paterfamilias: sipping iced tea, rocking contentedly on the back porch.

Eventually, and despite his antipathy toward insurance salespeople, Ron bought a small policy from me (and despite my qualms about transacting business with a neighbor who'd developed into a very personable friend). One night he asked me to come over to explore "an important question" facing him and his wife, Colleen. It was whether I thought he should leave his secure and rewarding position at Parker Steel, and if I thought he could run his own steel company. I answered by asking him two questions: "Are you really good at what you do?" and "Do you know the steel business?" When he answered both in the affirmative, I told him straightaway I believed he should do it. Poor Colleen. She'd obviously been fretting about what amounted to a risky proposition, when their lifestyle had been rolling along smoothly. And here I come along and give her husband a nudge that might tip the balance into eye-bulging debt and gut-wrenching uncertainty. While I could certainly sympathize with her legitimate concerns, I was also convinced that Ron was candid in his self-appraisal and that he was the type of man who could take on a whale of a challenge. He was and he did.

He went deeply into hock and had to take out a very substantial life insurance policy as a hedge against the indebtedness. But in only six months he proved he'd made the right move in setting up Stateline Steel. In the succeeding five years, Ron also became the most prolific referral source I ever had. Not only did he steadily increase his own insurance coverage and annuities, he also matched me with no fewer than 30 contacts representing as many as 100 clients. Most were either small-business owners or high-income professionals. I have to wonder about the outcome if Ron hadn't been intrigued at seeing Kate and our kids at their gardening . . . or if he had not taken that big leap into the unknown . . . or if I had fudged on my perception that I felt he was up to it.

In time, Stateline Steel was sold, with Ron taking over as president of a holding company for steel operations. I did my best to serve him to the fullest extent of my experience, which was well beyond the purview of an insurance salesman. He reciprocated. Again, I gained far more than I gave, including the friendship of an exceptional executive. Service is often its own reward, à la patience. Put both at the front of your tickler file.

... AND THE REFERRALS ROLL ON

Steel. Maybe it's split my persona. I've sure been heavily involved with that fascinating business via Ron Langenderfer, one of whose many referrals led me to John Bates, president and CEO of Heidtman Steel. John is possibly the most capable executive I've met at the head of a good-sized company. And talk about precocious: As an outsider, he took over the helm of the Heidtman family business at the tender age of 24 years! It's one of the largest steel processors in the United States. John's now 48. As a testament to his leadership, his employees voted against unionization by a margin of 220 to 4.

After Ron's introduction, I met John for lunch and found that he lived up to his reputation—tremendous selling ability, unlimited energy, a one-man band. After dining, he took me for a tour of his facility, displayed a business acumen that was virtually encyclopedic, practically monopolized the conversation (which I love, because I learn so much), then told me that Ron said he appreciated my advice and that maybe I could be of help to Heidtman Steel. During my tour, it became clear that John was as plain-spoken with his work force as his office was devoid of knick-knacks and frills. And I gathered that his office door was always open. In the course of our dialogue, John fielded ten interruptions. He was the eye of the storm and didn't reveal the slightest irritation over being kept constantly involved in minute-to-minute inquiries and their ensuing decisions. In fact, he gave the strong impression that he wanted every intrusion his people thought was called for, to be kept as up-to-date as possible—and forget the bother aspect. He exemplifies the entrepreneurial executive, who remains in close contact with his troops, as opposed to the run-of-the-mill exec in Humongous Inc., who's out of touch with the workers.

Along with getting to know John and his work style, I got my eyes opened as to what it meant to be in his kind of business. I couldn't believe I'd ever see that much steel ready to be processed—all kinds and sizes, a beehive of efficient activity. People moving steel.

For the two of us, at the outset, it was a slow prospect/agent relationship, which involved poking into the areas of wills and trusts. I asked him how I could be of help. He asked me to give a talk to his employees (Ron Langenderfer had clued John in on the potential of such an event). I spoke for an hour on employee personal development, positive attitude, stress relief, excitement for work, etc. That was followed by another address concentrating on the ins and outs of total financial planning. There was no fee for any of this.

John and I met for breakfast four times that first year, with broad discussions on company growth and direction, banking and a variety of development-related subjects. These unhurried, casual meanderings led to my becoming agent for all of the company's group insurance, coverage for executives' life insurance and referrals that tripled the volume of those transactions; John alone probably directed me to 20 prospects, with inevitable spin-offs from those. Like an atomic explosion, the expansion is exponential—ever-widening.

In a practical way, I was being rewarded for a method of operation: providing services the prospect needed but which were unrelated to an insurance sale, unrelated to insurance itself and for which I would not accept a penny in pay. I was paid only when a sale of insurance was effected. A unique way to sell? It is certainly another way to sell! But ponder the fact that there is really not all that much difference among the insurance coverages being offered in the marketplace. So if you are capable of doing so, why not provide something out of the ordinary— something that separates you from the rest of the herd? And when you're dealing at the corporate level, be mindful of the fact that it's far easier for a president to sign a company check than a personal one—and that corporate bank account is generally much, much larger.

Moving along . . . It's funny but instructive to note the various ways in which a salesperson can ply the trade, via all sorts of unexceptional initial contacts. In my case, as recited thus far, they involved a friend of the family, a neighbor talking over the fence, a high school classmate and a fellow lecturer sharing the same rostrum. Then there's sports, which meandered me toward two fabulous accounts.

TAKE ADVANTAGE OF TEAM SPIRIT

I first encountered Mike Cicak (on his way to becoming president of Glasstech Inc.) by way of fast-pitch softball. My acquaintance with Burt Rose (multiple businesses, especially fast-food operations) blossomed from our mutual affection for federation basketball—he as sponsor, me as a player.

Mike Cicak became my entree to Harold McMaster, Glasstech's chairman of the board, an internationally renowned physicist and prolific inventor. I met Harold ten years ago, when he was in his mid-60s. At that age, conventional wisdom would conclude that Harold had long since lined up all of his insurance, estate and trust ducks, and that prospects for a sale to him were absolutely nil. Right? *Wrong!* Put this at the top of your can-do bible: Age is no barrier to prospecting. Just the opposite! Harold McMaster became my number one client. Never assume that wealthy senior citizen status means a person is secure with total financial management, that he or she has a shrewd agent protecting and nurturing the nest-egg. That's a myth. The reality is that the seniors are in the best prospect category. They may have a pile of money; they may feel personally secure. But they also might, through misdirection, be paying grossly excessive taxes with money they would prefer to leave to their kids or grandchildren, and/or donate to worthy charities. There are also countless examples of seniors who were middle-class citizens through most of their lives and who, through dint of work or luck, suddenly find themselves with more money than they literally know what to do with, or do with most effectively (and legally). *That's* where a knowledgeable, alert agent can move in and make his client and himself some real windfalls.

EVEN GENIUSES NEED SOME HELP

Through a couple of get-acquainted sessions, I learned Harold's history . . . about frustrations early on, when big corporate mentalities could not keep up with his inventive intellect. The guy knew glass as did few others in the world—how to refine it, bend it and, later on, use it as a conduit for generating power. But he couldn't sell his pioneering notions. Too many nonscientific technicalities kept interfering. He was told he didn't appreciate the market-driven realities. So he cut loose on his own, eventually setting up a succession of companies. But, although he was a consummate scientist with a talent for converting his brain-power to practical applications, Harold readily admitted he was deficient in grappling with the business side of a business. In fact, he felt so keenly about the problems that he endowed an institute at Bowling Green State University with the aim of helping inventive scientists and business executives understand how each is supposed to function, and how they can and must learn to work together for the edification of both.

When Harold asked what my line of work was, I told him I sold insurance and that I helped businesses fine-tune their operations. For instance? he asked. I cited The Andersons. Harold called Dick Anderson. Two days later I got a call. Harold wondered if, for a fee, I'd go to a community in the region and check out someone Glasstech was considering for a top-level executive position. I said I'd be happy to do so, but that I would not accept a fee. After conducting the interview, I gave Harold my impressions, which matched his own. When Harold insisted he wanted to pay me, I demurred with my standard disclaimer: Maybe someday you'll want me for an insurance service; it's then that I'll take my pay (commission).

He then asked if I'd be willing to serve on an advisory board to Glasstech, with remuneration, of course. I replied that, yes, I'd serve— without pay. Two meetings hence, Harold told me "Dick [Anderson] said you do financial planning," and he invited me to speak on that subject to all of Glasstech's employees. I did so, gratis, at Owens Technical College, a neighbor of Glasstech's.

Next, Harold—who is extremely soft-spoken and very shy— asked if I'd fill his invitation to speak on the world economy before a gathering of farmers at Defiance College. I accepted, driving with Harold (4:45 a.m. start) for the 6 a.m. presentation. It was standing room only (northwest Ohio is heavy into sophisticated farming) and the reception was, in Harold's view, "terrific." Again, I declined his proffer of a gratuity because, I explained, it was not insurance-sale related.

By now Harold was ready to concentrate on what I was all about. Generous to a fault, Harold and his wife of 55 years, Helen, had been passing out gifts by the millions: to his beloved Defiance College (where he met Helen), to Bowling Green State University, to the University of Toledo, to public broadcasting—to almost everybody with a charitable hit list.

What a pair to exemplify the attraction of opposites! Harold, the epitome of ultraquiet reserve; Helen, the quintessential "Unsinkable Molly Brown," hitting the floor running at six o'clock in the morning and spinning like a dynamo until bedtime—thinking nothing of having 30 people over for a Thanksgiving feast (four children and a flock of grandkids at their remarkably modest home; no pretensions). The classic power behind the exceptionally successful man.

After I was asked to examine their financial package, it was immediately apparent where the fault lay in their massive generosity. The solution to what amounted to easily avoidable taxation, I explained, was through deferred gifting—life insurance policies which provided deferred gifts to the beneficiaries, with the insured paying out only the annual premiums. When I told Harold the cost vs. the alternative, he said, for openers, "I'd like two!" My commission that day was very rewarding. Quick on those heels came a cornucopia of commissioned services—estate tax planning (with multiple tax advantages), group coverage, insurance for executives, etc. Mike Cicak, my fast-pitch softball connection to Harold McMaster, became my personal client—and gave me 20 referrals to boot.

Where my sports-connected introduction to Mike Cicak/Harold and Helen McMaster/Glasstech goes back ten years, my association with the sports-connected Burt Rose spans more than three decades.

McDONALD'S: SERVICE WITH A SMILE

Burt appeared on the Toledo scene with partner Jerry Izon to open the first McDonald's restaurant here in 1959. Both were avid sports fans, sponsoring, as just one example, a federation basketball team on which I played.

Burt introduced me to "the legend," Ray Kroc, McDonald founder, a dyed-in-the-wool salesman and the very essence of the entrepreneurial spirit. Ray Kroc's perception of being educated was to get up early and work late. A high school dropout, he had little regard for higher education beyond the unique institution of his own creation. I was one of the first outside speakers he had at Hamburger University, the cradle of McDonald's management development. A number of speeches on the usual subjects were sprinkled over McDonald's franchises nationwide, perhaps 20. I followed the same procedure: no pay for those services.

Burt Rose and Jerry Izon signed up for $100,000 life insurance policies (not bad for those days). Scores of other McDonald's employees followed suit—so much so that, in the 1960s, my annual income from that sole source was $35,000.

But circumstances required me to bend my no-compensation rule for speech making. For example, McDonald's asked me to address its national convention in Phoenix. Here we were getting into an exceptional demand/time frame, for which I accepted a $5,000 fee. I've accepted other fees since then, but only when the invitation imposes a burden clearly beyond what I ordinarily encounter—and only within the budget of what a client is manifestly willing to offer.

DOCTORS: A PRESCRIPTION FOR SUCCESS

I'm going to wrap up this episode with another nugget I gleaned from a lifetime of prospecting: While seniors represent a fantastic sales opportunity as an age group, physicians constitute the best prospects among professionals. And if the salesperson and the doctor prospect happen to have large families, so much the better.

Why? Aside from being very highly educated, physicians have high average incomes, and they have an inordinate consciousness of the value of life insurance and disability income. They deal constantly with the inevitability of death. They also constitute a very select, tight fraternity in which news travels fast. They rely upon and trust one another's competence and sound judgment. They practically invented the phenomenon of referrals. They put a premium on integrity. Much is demanded of them; they demand much in return from those who hope to serve them. Characteristically, as a group, they detest quackery, within their midst or without. If you can enlist their confidence, you will have tapped into the heftiest life insurance consumer group of all the professions.

I began learning some of the above because a colleague left town. As what turned out to be a going-away present (to my benefit!), he introduced me to a storied pair of plastic surgeons, Drs. John Kelleher and Jim Sullivan. Among their many other distinctions, these partners established the first medical corporation of its kind in Ohio and pioneered a teaching clinic for plastic surgeons. Also, I had nine kids; John and Jim, ten and nine, respectively.

We hit it off beautifully from the beginning—they're beautiful guys. It started fast, with a review and upgrade of the Kelleher portfolio. Jim Sullivan followed in short order. Next came total financial planning. Referrals spilled over the transome—14 clients from their clinic alone.

Those physician antennae reach far and wide. An alumnus of the Kelleher/Sullivan clinic, Dr. Butch Kincaid, then at Wright-Patterson Air Field in Dayton, Ohio, matched me up with a pal, Dr. Larry Weininger, who was coming here to look for a home. As a measure of how we've since gotten along, I've involved Larry in 14 partnerships with which I've been engaged, including partnership in The Andersons and in Burger King's Baltimore restaurants.

Several other doctors formed the bedrock of my involvement with members of the medical profession, at a time when we were all much younger: Dr. Paul Raglow, father of nine—I became his first contact in Toledo, by way of a recommendation from a friend in Cleveland; Drs. Dick Torchia and Tom Abood, with whom I've been involved in numerous financial activities beyond insurance; and Dr. Ray Buganski, father of 11, a very close friend over the years. Each one is an exemplary, respected physician, wonderful spouse and parent, durable client and bountiful source of referrals. They and so very many others in my acquaintance have demonstrated the truism that you can have a wonderful life instigated by your career and that you really can avoid the obnoxious and worse by zeroing in on the class acts. Great friendships, as with a great job, are worth the effort. Give them, and it, all you've got.

10

Recruiting New Agents

As a very young insurance salesman in my twenties, I failed miserably. Oh, I had the desire and the enthusiasm. I was reasonably intelligent. But I had more "caller reluctance" than you could weigh on a flatbed. I was so inexperienced and immature that I didn't realize such was normal for my age and position. Worse, my break-in trainer, although a very good person who was genuinely interested in my welfare, was neither a top salesman nor an effective mentor. He simply lacked sales instruction skills. That I survived at all was clearly a matter of by guess and by golly. I was a mediocrity who lasted. The pressure was lessened, however, by virtue of the fact that I did not partake of the sacrament of matrimony until I was 29 years of age.

Like most of my colleagues past and present, I liked, and like, selling insurance. Those who abandoned it, in my opinion, did so because they could not learn fast enough to survive. They wanted to stay but could no longer afford to do so.

A BETTER WAY BEGINS WITH EDUCATION

That painful introduction to selling, along with decades of close observation of salespeople, taught me some powerful lessons. They can be summarized in two words: selection and training. And much of both, in my opinion, goes against the grain in corporate practice and in higher education. So many in both of those camps simply don't know what's going on—or, if they do, don't know how to fix it.

You know there must be a better way to successful selling. I can tell from the virtually universal reaction—the nods of approval—when I give a speech and say there's *got* to be a more effective way to select and train a sales force than the prevailing mish-mash. Ironically, many in higher education agree. I know; I've spoken on the subject at scores of universities, in serious conferences with presidents and deans and assistant deans of business colleges. A few have a smattering of sales courses. Upon examination, I found those courses to be far below acceptability. One was actually pathetic, as are most of the texts on salesmanship. Nobody disagrees when I contend that the colleges must institute a full-blown degree in sales. They concur that the need is evident. They even have a number of courses that could blend in nicely with a sales degree major. But they don't have a clue as to how such a sales degree should be implemented. (I was actually offered the opportunity to inaugurate such a degree program—if I would head it up. I declined.) What a wonderful thing it would be if Company X could send a representative to a college campus and have him or her be able to recruit a covey of newly minted graduates, each with a sales diploma, trained by knowledgeable professors and a team of sales professionals who would serve as part-time instructors and advisers! It's certainly do-able. It's definitely needed. And what a head start for the kids! It's plain crazy that it hasn't long since been put into effect. It's *got* to come.

Without the benefit of a higher education degree program in sales, we continue to see the pervasive mentality—dictated from the corporate hierarchy and absorbed by the troops—that perpetuates the "buyer beware" syndrome: a sales force constantly violating the consumer's neutral zone—obnoxious in its persistence, impatient, oblivious to building an appreciative, loyal clientele. Rather than striving to treat the buyer as Number One, it's "make the sale" and let tomorrow take care of itself.

Companies appear to be obsessed with stamping out a ready-made sales team of older, "seasoned" members. They want "experience" and "maturity"—without bothering to develop the *selling* capabilities that go with those terms. They want the guy in his thirties, wife and two kids, a "stable" man—or a woman in her thirties with "presence," attractive, with a fine command of the language. Then they lump these thirty-something salespeople together under a manager who has no appreciation of sales dynamics. Frequently, their boss is a nice mediocrity who's been moved into management—i.e., he or she has failed upward.

In the early stages, they constantly assemble for sales meetings, mostly oriented toward product knowledge (enough to fill an elephant). Typically, after the initial few weeks, the sales force is pretty much left to drift on its own in terms of direct supervision and training. As a replacement, a continuous stream of reports flows from salesmen to their boss, thence up the line to the vice president of such-and-such. A paper chase instead of a deliberate prospect chase. They are told how to dress, nudged into making social contacts with prospects at a fancy country club, given parameters on what kind of car to drive . . . all sorts of guidance, except for the kind that delineates how to successfully prospect for sales and cement a clientele. It is a thinking process geared to the short haul—from businesses that otherwise expect to be around for a long time. What a thoroughly mixed-up contradiction.

SOME NEW THOUGHTS ON SELECTION AND TRAINING

Given the best of all worlds, let's say that, out of the blue, I was put in charge of an ideal division of 40 salespeople. Among other things, I would have the authorization to pick their age groupings, unrealistic as all this would be. Still, I want to illustrate my point. So, I'd have ten people in their twenties, ten in their thirties, ten in their forties and ten in their fifties. The older personnel would be selected for obvious reasons. The exception lies with those youngsters in their twenties—the ones too many companies don't even consider. They don't want to waste their time and *money* on bringing youth along—let 'em learn someplace else, then come see us when they're "ready." Me, I'd *concentrate* on those 20-year-olds, knowing that the best of the lot wouldn't really be into a selling mode for at least five years, maybe even ten. That time element is crucial. They've got to be given time to fall on their faces, get up, dust themselves off and, with proper training, get back on track. They must not be dismissed for "not getting the job done." They're too young to know how to get the job done! But they will know, if given the time and proper instruction. That's how you build sales force continuity—and competence: the mature bringing along the immature.

Selection, to me, focuses on attracting bright, well-educated men and women in their early twenties, because if I mean to stay in business for a long time, I know I cannot train over a short period of time. Trying to recruit instant wizards, to get orders *now,* runs counter to the long-term philosophy. Of course, there may be that exceptional youngster who does well right off the bat. In corporate America, the reaction would probably be to just leave the kid alone. My reaction would be to continually supervise and train that exception, as I would all the others, and look forward to him or her tripling his or her sales results. I'm convinced that close, individual supervision and training are basic to any effective sales operation, day after day. I also know that failures for even the most gifted go with the game. Every salesperson is constantly confronted with failure. Failure is a test, as is success. They are both hurdles in an individual's development. The younger the salesperson, the greater the challenges inherent in those hurdles, and the greater the need for effective mentoring. They need time to realize that winning is never final and that losing is never fatal. They can't simply hear these truths; they have to live them—by being trained *every day* and then turned loose to do their thing; not with classes and reams of reports, but with one-on-one dialogue. Skip the memos. Give me eyeball-to-eyeball, all the time. And let me tell you, it's a great pleasure to teach young people. I've relished doing so for more than 30 years. Their victories become your victories.

"YOUR OWN THING" MAY BE JUST THAT

Somehow, many sales managers have been convinced that, because times (and people) have changed, it's alright to bring in a young fellow with a ring in his ear, hair well below the collar and generally unkempt. He's "doing his own thing," or "he's exercising his civil rights." To a sales effort, he's also akin to a torpedo on the loose. He may be intellectually brilliant and mama's pride and joy. But in my studied judgment, his public will perceive him as someone who, if not to be disdained outright, will certainly not be taken seriously—a maverick who cares more about his appearance than he does about bare-bones reality. Pete the Tramp can boast, "I did it my way." That's why he dresses the way he does; that's why he's a tramp.

The same goes for the young lady whose hair makes her look as though she has two heads, one atop the other, wears half the makeup of a beauty salon and lurches along on spike heels.

Sure, either or both could beat what I'd rate as prohibitive odds; but they'd be unmitigated exceptions to the odds and to common sense.

Let's say it got down to a wager: One group of 15 young college graduate trainees is characterized as "with it"; lots of hair, jewelry, "expressive" clothing. Also, let's say they were bright young people. Another group of 15 bright young sales aspirants is well-groomed and conservatively dressed. Flat out, I'd bet the latter group would easily outproduce the former bunch in any legitimate sales effort short of peddling the hippie look—which brings to mind a favored expression: You can't make a chicken salad out of chicken feathers.

Further, my personal slant is that you're a winner in the sartorial–personal grooming contest if nobody really notices your get-up. In that event, you're probably well-groomed. To that I'll add that everyone in sales management has the right to choose who they want or need in their organization. They have the right to exclude the oddballs whose very appearance—without their saying one word—can be a first-impression (lasting) prospect turnoff. A sales manager is under absolutely no compulsion to shoot himself in his own foot, the cry of "civil rights" notwithstanding. Too often that protestation is nothing more than an excuse to thumb one's nose at society—an exercise in egotism and self-indulgence. It is not the hallmark of a sales effort geared to attending the needs—and sensibilities—of its clientele. It's not "buyer beware"; it's seller beware. Go after the clean-cut, All-American look that's identifiable with educated, enthusiastic, highly trainable, want-to-learn youth. Then make sure that they maintain that persona—that they do not go to seed. Mandate neatness; prohibit ostentation. We're not in beauty—or ugly—contests. We're in the very serious enterprise of guiding people around financial landmines.

And I'm hoping that the training in my beloved insurance industry (and any other that may profit from this reading) will improve markedly over the poor grade I would accord it at present. Let's select well and then change the training.

11

In Search of Training

The problems in training for the insurance industry do not start at the home office. Don't say "Home offices don't know what they're doing when it comes to training." I hate to say it, but that's not their job. Granted, I've said repeatedly that home offices aren't very effective in giving sales ideas. But those have to come from practitioners in the trenches—on the front lines in areas of both training and generating ideas. That's the beauty of the underwriter associations across the country—and of the Million Dollar Round Table, whose exchange of ideas put me where I am in the insurance industry. Again, training cannot be done in the home office; training must be done in the field.

An important consideration: There is not just *one* way to effective training. But ask yourself this: Have you been well trained, or was it a matter of natural instinct and skills that got you where you are? Is your degree of success *attributable* to training—or in spite of it?

This is not meant to disparage those who are great trainers, or to throw brick-bats at those who have been anything but. I'm riding at this point on input I've received over literally decades of speaking all over the country and the world, and from follow-up correspondence.

Cumulatively, the verdict has been overwhelming: The training received runs the gamut from inadequate to counterproductive. It bringS to mind Thoreau's melancholy observation about most men living lives of quiet desperation. How much of our misery is self-imposed, and how much is inflicted by others? Often, the desperation is a result of both. I contend that both afflictions can be reduced significantly for most of us, if not totally eliminated.

In the professional realm, the constructive training phase begins with the goal of making us more effective and productive, taking greater pride in and deriving more happiness from what we do to make a living. OK, then, just what do I think has to be changed?

DEVELOPING A CLIENTELE

To get down to practicalities, I'll start with the recurring answer I receive when I pose this question to underwriters: Does your office have a system that routinely kicks in the names of clients who are up for what should be an annual review? Eight of ten reply in the negative; six of ten say annual reviews were never brought up in their training. If service is the name of the game, there is *no way* you can keep up with your clientele if you do not, at least once a year, initiate direct contact! First, build a relationship, then *develop* a clientele. That's the *rule numero uno*. Most who succeed do so with and through existing clients. Trainers, take heed: Make that the cornerstone of your instruction.

Next, trainers, do yourselves and your vulnerable, innocent trainees the priceless service of burying forever the death-defying cold call, be it by telephone or by knocking on a door. Make them "frozen" calls: Put 'em on ice forever in the deepest freezer you can find. Conjure up an image of the punch-drunk fighter who had a lifetime of cold calls. Broken nose, cauliflower ears, scar tissue around the eyes and cheekbones, bells ringing, shadow-boxing when there ain't no shadow. That's the figurative fate awaiting the poor, misguided contender who stakes his career on cold calls on frigid prospects. I consign it to the category of too-tough-on-the-brain. It is a fate rampant with fear and trepidation, and one that is minimally productive. I say, for the zillionth time, use the referral method—using one satisfied client as an entree to a prospect. For the new agent, start with cultivating your friends and acquaintances, then get them to open up access to *their* friends and acquaintances. If you've served your initial clients well, they'll be pleased to make referrals in your behalf. Left far behind will be the manipulator of the cold call.

Sure, there are those who will say cold calls "are what put me in the business." To which I say, bless you. I'm here to sympathize with and try to protect, among others, the bright young college grad who has everything going for him, who is weighed, evaluated, then signed on as an insurance agent trainee. Soon, his "indoctrination" includes an order to call on 50 small businesses within the next 30 days. Quit laughing; some miserables are actually run through that kind of idiot's maze—which helps account for an overwhelming dropout rate. They're virtually directed to fail.

It's as self-destructive as the hiring of professionals from other insurance companies who are given the title and mission of personal producing general agents. They neither recruit nor train, just produce for their own company. That route follows the one taken by the dinosaurs.

I now have an inkling of what John the Baptist must have felt when he wondered if anyone would hear the word he was trying to spread. I've been trying for decades to impart what I've absorbed from countless counselings with young insurance practitioners, people I enjoy training and to whom I am only too happy to transfer ideas. And what I've absorbed from all that communication is the conviction of an overriding need to get back to the recruitment and effective training of top-flight people. Earlier I wrote that home offices cannot be blamed for training that must be conducted in the field. However, to the home offices I say this: For all your commendable high integrity and many contributions to the growth of our industry and nation, what you've been doing isn't enough. You must set aside a very substantial amount of money for education and for assistance to the trainers who are in the field. These funds can be used to examine every avenue of training, to demand high performance, to encourage people like Tom Wolff in creating up-to-date training methods. I've long been a fan of Tom's— and others of his breed who spend a lot of time trying to turn novices into real insurance professionals.

While we're at it, let's throw the direct mail dinosaur into the same deep freeze with the cold call. Direct mail translates to massive amounts of money for piddling amounts of return from a public searching for responsible fiscal leadership. Yeah, I can hear it now—the plaintive excuse that "at least direct mail gives them a track to run on." Sure, and they're just as productive as the tracks running through abandoned towns, leading to nowhere.

Or "direct mail provides an activity for new agents." Drones have activity; but where's the *product*ivity?

THE PRODUCER-TRAINER: A WINNING HYBRID

What of the practitioner who is a top producer but who cannot teach, or the agent who is no fireball as a producer but makes an excellent instructor? I'd agree 100 percent with anyone who makes a point in behalf of either or both of those individuals. And add this: Those are exceptions. I'm looking for agents who can produce *and* teach. Of course, they have to care, be truly interested in the other person and produce irrespective of the degree of compensation they receive for teaching. I felt so strongly about this when I built my agency in Toledo, Ohio, that no one could be a trainer if he or she wasn't a producer. Later on I adopted a related precondition: To be on our executive staff, you have to be a member of the Million Dollar Round Table. The results are in; the organization has grown. It's better now with my brother, Bob, at the helm than it was 17 years ago when I was in charge; it's ten times its former size. Bob's a top administrator. I'm a teacher who happened to have enjoyed building the agency. Our trainers of today are members of the Million Dollar Round Table. None relies on overrides of the new people to make a living. If they all quit training today, they'd earn more income starting tomorrow by increasing their personal production.

As I've been a maverick in the selection process, in targeting the 21- to 25-year-olds as prime sales trainees, I'm also "different" (and have been hugely successful) in a key aspect of their training. Thirty-two years ago, I introduced the (then) almost unheard of process of teaching trainees in the intricacies of total financial planning. This entailed a coincidental eccentricity: I start that vital lesson by teaching them how to manage their own money. That total financial planning strategies are an invaluable asset to an insurance agent is inarguable. And no one is in a better position to profit from such knowledge than an insurance agent.

TRAINEES GO FOR THE GOLD

But it seems axiomatic to me that before guiding a client in money management, the agent must first have his or her own financial house in order. And that's the rule I set in concrete. To my fledgling sales-people I say, have $10,000 in savings within three years. In other words, I'm not teaching theory; this is reality. It's an irreplaceable discipline. And I drive the point home time and again . . . à la the pro, Jimmy Cromb, who introduced me to golf. Instead of the conventional "good-bye," "so long" or "see you later," Jimmy adopted this unique phrase: "Slow back." It was a patented farewell, but it was also his way of reinforcing the necessity of a golfer swinging his or her club back slowly and deliberately before hitting the ball. Similarly, my young trainees soon learn that my greeting is more than a vacant "Hello." I habitually pose the question, "How's your 10 doing?" They know I want to know how their savings are piling up. They're also aware they'll get that inquiry until they accumulate that $10,000. Sure, I'm aware that the figure could justifiably rise, what with inflation. But I'm not out to teach numbers in the Consumer Price Index. I'm out to teach self-discipline. And there is no substitute for the personal struggle that goes with building one's own nest-egg. It's also a wonderful way to build pride, a sense of real accomplishment.

My trainees are told they can meet the savings goal by sticking to the basics. Sure, you need a car; it's essential for transportation. But it doesn't necessarily have to be a new car, and certainly not one that's big and costly. There are other, more historic needs: food, clothing and shelter. What is counterproductive is the mindset that prescribes any-thing elaborate in what you eat, wear or live in. And young and old have to set aside a modest sum for an earned vacation. It needn't be a long, fashionable jaunt; that's for those who have it made. For the young sales aspirant, a week or so at a reasonably priced lake cottage will do the trick. It's a matter of distinguishing between want versus need—and suppressing the wants. I went through plenty of those hoops; mine is not a case of "do what I say, don't do what I did." Wife Kate and I kept it Spartan simple when I was a 29-year-old newlywed. We lived above a drugstore on Door Street in Toledo, Ohio. The first three years, we saved half our meager income (while we were rearing three children). We didn't go "out" to movies, dinners, plays and the like. Our idea of a great evening was to stay home, grill a steak, enjoy each other's company and that of several close friends whose entertainment was good conversation. I felt I had solid priorities: 12-hour workdays; no frills. But I didn't work Friday evenings, Saturdays or Sundays. Sunday was and is the Lord's day, which includes morning Mass and the rest of the day relaxing.

Over the last five years, I've managed to redeem a pledge that Kate does not cook on Sunday (other than an extremely rare exception). We go to a restaurant for Sunday breakfast and, often as not, split a store-bought pizza for dinner. We did it all and then some, thanks to a great marriage partner who shared the same principles and objectives.

THE LOST ART OF LISTENING

Discipline—a marvelous trait—also encompasses keeping one's mouth shut at the appropriate times. Too many in sales are not hard of hearing, they're hard of *listening!* To be successful in sales, you've got to be a good listener. That's why, before meeting with a client or prospect, I stress the importance of "mental rehearsal." I turn off the radio and tune out all other distractions to concentrate fully on the impending meeting, reminding myself of the ground to be covered. And the first hard rule for any such engagement is to devote the first 15 or 20 minutes to listening to what my guest has to say. Let the client or prospect do all the initial talking; let him or her control the conversation. If you listen, they'll tell their needs soon enough. Don't ever fall into the trap of being surprised at what you learn—that is, that what they say is contrary to what you expected. It's not your province to assume. Your listening is the preamble to client/prospect dialogue—the power that unveils the wherewithal for a solid discussion of total financial planning. Conversely, if you act impatiently, monopolize the conversation or operate with a canned presentation, the odds will have you talking to someone who is figuratively deaf—on another planet so far as what you've saying. Be smart. Listen first.

So I want to get more and more people thinking about constructive training. And I don't want to hear about training until I hear about results. I'm results-oriented. The results say it all. Contrary to what I've heard all my life, the proof is not in the pudding; the proof of the *pudding* is in the *eating*.

12

Everything but a Sales Degree

Any reader of this book will discern that I have bones to pick with major corporations and higher education. This chapter will serve to define the basis for my criticisms of those two powerful entities, so far as the sales profession is concerned. And, while they're anything but dead horses, I'm going to continue to beat on them.

First, let's look at what I consider to be some fascinating—and damning—statistics. According to the 1990 U.S. census, the number of people actually employed in sales positions of one capacity or another totaled a whopping 14,192,000. That's slightly more than 12 percent of everybody aged 16 years and older who has a job. To put that stupendous total in an even more illuminating light, you could take all of our primary- and secondary-school teachers (3,994,000); every secretary, stenographer and typist (4,654,000); all of the 4,492,000 engaged in our massive health-care system; and then tack on the 864,000 who work as mathematical and computer scientists, and you'd end up with a combined 14,004,000—still well below our total sales contingent.

Let me emphasize: I'm talking about professional salespeople, not the kid swapping an apple for a cookie, or the millions who peddle their own houses, cars, boats and anything else that can be funneled through a garage sale. Selling—professional and amateur—is not only the oldest but also the most ubiquitous of occupations.

THE ASTONISHING GROWTH OF SALES

And those of us in professional sales in the United States have been busy, especially since the end of World War II. For example, final sales volume in the fourth quarter of 1946 was a comparatively slim $15.8 billion. It took 28 years, until 1974's fourth quarter, to top $100 billion (specifically, $104.6 billion), but only six more years—until 1980's fourth—to hit $201.1 billion. In another six years, by 1986, the last quarterly mark weighed in at $389.6 billion, within easy shooting distance of the $400 billion level—a more than 25-fold increase since the year Japan and Germany threw in the towel. Granted, population growth and inflation played important roles. And, certainly, so did affluence. Heck, when I was growing up during and in the wake of World War II, most of us didn't have a garage in which to hold a sale. Even if someone did, there was virtually nothing to peddle; we made do with what we had. Anything disposable went into the junk heap.

But then, almost miraculously, the Big Party began. The early 1950s ushered in the terrible Korean War, along with an almost unimaginable improvement in incomes and lifestyles. A parade of new products came on line, à la television, and millions of us—for the first time—had pockets sufficiently deep to indulge a lot of our fancies. The two-car family became commonplace. Behind that pattern of conspicuous consumption was a high-powered manufacturing capability, a worldwide demand (to a militarily victorious nation) and a growing army of salespeople, the vast majority of whom learned their vital trade in as haphazard and ill-considered a process as one could ever encounter. Looking back on our history of sales professionalizing, I have to conclude that our growth in sales has been more a matter of fortunate coincidence than competence. We had a hammerlock on an international seller's market—a virtual paradise for order-takers. Along the way, neither buyer nor seller was well-served.

THE FAILURE OF CORPORATE AMERICA
AND ACADEMIA

Now that the Big Party's over and our nation's economic survival is on the line, we have to face the stark reality that our sales force, generally, is ill-equipped to toe the line. Nowhere is the blame for that deficiency more appropriately placed than with our institutions of higher learning—and with the corporate giants who bend their ear and who, ironically, constitute less than 1 percent of the nation's employers!

Let's consider that the United States has 3,200 two- and four-year colleges. Collectively, they offer 64 major fields of study by discipline, from agribusiness and agricultural production to zoology, with a catch-all of first professional degrees—e.g., chiropractic, dentistry, law. Now, under those 64 study umbrellas are a prodigious 490 subheadings or areas of concentration. These include the familiar accounting, biology and business economics, and the not-so-familiar equestrian science, jazz folklore and mythology, tourism and peace studies.

Each year more than 9.3 million students are enrolled in those courses. Each year more than a million collect their bachelor or first professional degree. But get this: Not one will have been educated specifically for a trade (sales) in which 12 percent of the employed are engaged and which constitutes the linchpin for hundreds of billions of dollars in transactions and uncountable other dollars in unrealized deals (emphasis on the latter). In short, if you want to be taught how to be a professional salesperson, don't look to a college or university—or to just about any major corporation or government-funded program, for that matter.

HAS AMERICA ABANDONED ITS WORKERS?

Speaking of the latter, a 1986 congressional study concluded that of the millions of disadvantaged and displaced workers, it is likely that no more than 5 percent are being served. That came on the heels of a federal job training program trend that saw a 65 percent cut between

1980 and 1988, from $10.8 billion to $5.6 billion. Our U.S. investment in government education and job training is a paltry 0.5 percent of the federal budget; Sweden's is 20 percent. France makes employers spend 1 percent of their profits on training their own workers, or they must contribute to a national training fund. Even Singapore reportedly spends 6 percent of its gross national product on job training.

American business isn't any great shakes, either. When surveyed by *Fortune* magazine in 1990 on what is the most important step American government or business can take to improve the quality of the U.S. work force, the top answer (64 percent) said "improve education." A far second was "expand training for employees" (11 percent). Incidentally, "address dissolution of the family" mustered only a 3 percent response.

Look at a June 1990 *Business Week* commentary by John Hoerr (including quotes from the Commission on Skills of the American Workforce):

> . . . business by and large is not demanding—and society is not delivering—the large-scale improvements in education and training that American industry needs . . . The transition from school to work in the United States is described as the worst of any industrialized society . . . Instead of investing in workers, most companies are pursuing other strategies to remain competitive: cutting wages, exporting production jobs to low-wage countries or de-skilling jobs through automation.

It's been reliably estimated that U.S. companies spend more than ten times as much on capital improvements as they do on worker training.

Two more quick but revealing quotes: from Coke CEO Robert Goizueta—"The long and short of it is that in education we may be encouraging mediocrity"—and from Nabisco CEO Louis V. Gerstner, Jr.: "The biggest risk in education is in not taking one."

TAKING ON THE ACADEMIC
BUREAUCRACY

Keep that quote, and its predecessors, in mind as I reveal the gist of interviews I conducted with senior administrators, at three of the numerous colleges and universities I visited, concerning the subject of structuring a degree program centering on sales. None offers a sales degree. Many appear to be interested, but the obstacles they tick off are seemingly beyond count. It makes me wonder how they ever got around to having majors in mythology and folklore studies, peace studies, equestrian studies, etc.

Anyway, I was given to understand that at a public institution, there is an awesome bureaucracy that must be pacified, convinced and otherwise recruited in order to undertake any significant new educational step. Start with a legislature and governor; then to a higher education controlling body, such as a board of regents; thence to the institution's trustees, president, administrative staff, deans, department chairpersons and professors. Staggering amounts of red tape glued to the fundamental of government-riddled realities: If you want us to give you a pile of money year after year, expect our noses and then some to be in your tent. Most of them *ought* to be aware that hordes of new business-college grads are having an increasingly tough time finding a job, and will continue to have a tough time. Young people who, as students, should have been looked upon as the most valuable persons in their respective schools and who sought—and seek—an education to enhance their chances for gainful employment are in dire need of enlightened, innovative assistance. Yet it's my impression that nobody at the top of either state government, colleges or college governing bodies thinks it's important to change, enhance or add to a curriculum to enable the creation of a sales degree—a degree that would give kids a big leg up on the sales position—filling demands that are going to escalate from here on out. And please forgive me, but marketing is not selling.

As I see it, a big part of the problem rests with the major universities getting their information on curriculum enhancement from the major corporations, most of which have experienced mass declines in employment. To reiterate a vital point: More than 99 percent of our jobs depend on small business.

Pardon a digression: I didn't know the original Henry Ford, but I know he was a salesman and an entrepreneur. I do know Bob Stranahan, whose father and uncle created Champion Spark Plug Company from a small beginning. Their salesmanship convinced a skeptical world that they had a product to be reckoned with. We need that kind of sales moxie and drive today. There's no room for the cigar-chomping, hail-fellow-well-met who thinks he can charm his way to a sale.

So, here's a wake-up call to the colleges and universities: Instead of going to the majors to discover society's ever-changing business needs, go to the small and midsize shops, where they face do or die every day of their existence; where they have maybe 15 on their force, with two of them selling; where they make, sell, deliver, collect—do everything on a shoestring and with no hope of a government bailout if they go belly-up.

As I was saying earlier, here's a synopsis of my treks to three significant universities out of many visited with wife Kate.

School No. 1

Midwestern public university with approximately 50,000 students (not Ohio State). My contact, the dean of the college of business administration, was a very bright and pleasant person. We reviewed my proposal for a sales degree. It developed that many of the supporting or complementary courses already existed—i.e., English and English literature, public speaking, interpersonal and other communication, business—but nothing in sales course hours. He discussed the bureaucratic obstacles referred to earlier, then laid this on me: "John, I cannot find one thing wrong with your recommendation except for the word 'selling'. It has a bad connotation. Let's work out a substitute word— and then sell it." Short pause. Then he said, "I can't believe what I just said." Neither could I; nor could I accept his proffered solution. I refuse to engage in double-speak or scout around for substitutes for the real thing. I can understand how some academics will switch the title from "home economics" to "applied human ecology" in the hope of broadening the scope of what pertains to them (although I don't know of any nonacademic who, at first glance, would understand what "applied human ecology" is all about without a descriptive program). No, selling is selling is selling. It's an important word, a meaningful and descriptive word. It needs no explanation or apologies or euphemism. I bade a sad farewell to Enormous University.

School No. 2

This visitation was shorter and far less encouraging. Our host at this public-supported university of roughly 18,000 students was the assistant dean of the business college. Once I got around to my mission— i.e., stumping for a college-level degree in sales to better enable his students to be gainfully employed, he stopped me short with this: "You must understand, our job is not to prepare students for employment." To which I responded, "Would you hold it right there? You know what you've just told me: Your job is not serving, it's being served." Imagine! That university's job—in the opinion of a key spokesperson—is not to prepare students to get a job! Rather, it is to throw out information, improve skills . . . and leave it at that. I left in a hurry, wondering among other things what the poor folks in the university employment placement office would think of such a philosophy. Cross-purposes, maybe?

School No. 3

Midsize, private and one of the most prestigious universities in the nation. The bureaucratic influence isn't as formidable in a private school as it is in one that's public. Still, there is no dearth of hurdles to curricular change. In meetings that totaled five hours during a two-day visit, I encountered dialogue that could fill a book. It was interesting and informative—an eye-opener. But the hesitancy toward significant change, even without state government looking over the shoulder, makes the sales degree dream still that. Great concern was expressed on the matter of where acceptable teachers could be obtained. I suggested that there are highly successful sales leaders and CEOs through-out the country, in small to midsize companies (who are themselves top salespeople) who would willingly accept invitations to teach, say, one course per semester for a period of three years. They'd consider doing so a unique gift to education and an intriguing change of pace from their workaday world. They'd introduce a breath of fresh air in any university fortunate enough to enlist them. Thoughtful members of the faculty would welcome them with open arms, in my judgment. How-ever, those concerned with their own turf might have a problem accepting "outsiders" who have the liability of having fought and won in the real world of selling and making a business prosper.

It didn't fly. While, with the glaring exception of School No. 2, there's wide agreement that a degree in sales (or some substitute title!) would be a desirable objective, there's also no sense of urgency to undertake the task. For want of a better analogy, it's like the blind leading the blind: big corporations that haven't a clue on how sales should be conducted and sales trainees trained, mentoring major colleges and universities on what business courses they should teach. The big losers are the kids hoping to get a job in business. I'll continue to press for that sales degree as long as I'm able. Perhaps one of you will then grasp the baton.

A CASE OF DIMINISHING RETURNS

Heaven knows we taxpayers, parents, students and donors spend a mind-marinating bundle of money on higher education. Altogether we shelled out $143.2 billion to colleges and universities for the school year ended in 1990—$92.2 billion to public and $51 billion to private institutions.

And, while taxes and donations account for a hefty share of the tab, the dollar burden on kids and their families gets more punitive by the quarter. Consider: The average cost for a resident student at a four-year public college in the 1990-91 school year was $6,991. For the young person going to a private school, the bite was $15,318. Start with a freshman at those levels and, what with inflation, the price tag on tuition, fees, books, supplies, room, board, transportation and miscellaneous expenses will—come graduation day—exceed $28,000 for the public college student and $60,000 for his or her private-school counterpart.

Ironically and unfortunately, while the campus-bound and their tax-laden supporters cough up progressively more, they're getting progressively less by way of exploding class sizes and diminishing exposure to high-priced professors, whose preoccupation with research has them palming off their teaching responsibilities to lower-paid and less experienced assistants. It wasn't like that when I went to college in the late 1940s and early 1950s; I had magnificent teachers—nary an assistant in the bunch. And many of them were also noted for their research! Let me say this: "Research" in many disciplines has become an unconscionable scam. Want proof? Scan the yards and yards of summaries on what's going on in the name of research at You-Name-It University, especially in the non-science-related disciplines. Education: many reams of "awful." Communications: many more "awfuls." Social sciences: ditto. Tens of millions of dollars for certifiable garbage. Is there any college president out there who wants to debate this?

So, as you may have gathered by now, there's a lot more stuck in my craw than simply the impediments against the introduction of a college-level degree in sales. The degree-inclined are financially discouraged and academically shortchanged by a system that balks at implementing a job-generating degree program to professionalize one of our national economy's most indispensable elements—selling, without which nothing moves.

13

In-laws, Outlaws and Passing on the Business

All right, the title above is a play on words, probably a limp attempt to inject a bit of playfulness or humor into the subject at hand. But there's nothing funny, in my opinion, about getting one's children into one's business act. Doing so creates a scenario that most often ends in anything but the pride and harmony originally anticipated. Far more often than not, the product is dissension, jealousy and failure—of familial relationships as well as the business.

I love my kids, all nine of them. But as soon as they were able to comprehend what I was saying, I told them flat out that they would not become part of my business enterprise. It's not that they aren't up to the challenge of the kind of work I'm in (they've already proven their capabilities); it's because I don't want them or me to fall into the treacherous pit my experiences have proven is potentially there.

Sure, there are the exceptions, where sons and/or daughters have come into dad's and/or mom's business, and business has boomed. But I also believe a geometric factor comes into play: The bigger the operation, the more family members that go into it, the greater the likelihood of disappointment, dissatisfaction and disaster. As notable exceptions, the aforementioned Andersons come quickly to mind. Successive bunches of kids and grandkids have grown within and with the firm. The same goes for Sauder Woodworking Company, a thriving mainstay in Archbold, Ohio. There, successive generations of Sauders have built a worldwide reputation for hardy, inexpensive furniture.

But for every such instance of beating the odds, I know of scores that succumbed to them. And, for all the confidence I have in my kids' abilities, I would not want to run such a risk—nor would I want to subject them to the extraordinary pressures of joining "the family business."

ALL IN THE FAMILY: TRIALS AND TRIBULATIONS

Let's itemize those pressures.

One day it's the Joe Doakes Company. The next it's Doakes & Son. Papa is pleased as punch that Junior is working for him—and immediately begins to compensate for the lad. Maybe the sheltering isn't patently deliberate; it's just an instinctual thing—dad doesn't want his boy to fall on his face. Nonetheless, any kid's shortcomings are bound to emerge. When they do, unless papa has the patience of Job (few do), he'll start applying the heat. In time, good old dad starts being looked upon as a budding ogre by sonny boy—then overpowering and dictatorial.

The son suddenly intuits that if the business prospers, it's the old man's doing; but if it flops, the child gets the donkey's tail pinned on him. It's the old saw about winners having plenty of parents and losers being orphans. The same script can be adapted to the husband/wife team that brings the child into the business fold. But now you have both parents in the supervisory act. Each could have far different attitudes on how the kid should progress. For example, dad may decide that Junior just can't cut the mustard and relay that message to mama. She could recognize it as stark if sad reality—or get on a high horse, tell papa he doesn't know what he's talking about and upbraid him for disparaging their wunderkind!

Then, when more than one child is admitted to the family business, there's the element of sibling rivalry. Here the kids are not only competing against each other in making themselves valuable to a company, they're also competing to maintain their position in the family's pecking order and in the esteem of their parents. Even if the tensions don't surface (a rarity), keeping them bottled up can be equally debilitating. Siblings are natural rivals—which, if contained, is healthy. But it can become very unhealthy when mixed into a family enterprise.

And just consider the possibilities for disaffection when the children bring their spouses into the family business proceedings. Even if the husband or wife of a child who joins the family's business stays outside the operation, that doesn't mean he or she cannot or will not criticize from the sidelines or make negative comparisons among relatives. Seldom is the air more charged in such an atmosphere than when the family business leader dies, and the acrimonious battle begins over who's going to assume the throne. All those in-law jokes didn't simply materialize from thin air. There's real substance to the timeworn stories about the battle-axe mother-in-law, the scrounging brother-in-law, etc. And pity the "winner." He or she may wear the crown, but if everything doesn't come up roses, or the business goes under, who will stick around long enough to pick up the pieces? More than likely, the losers will figuratively bombard the successor with every rock in the playground.

There's also a tricky sidebar to getting a youngster active in a parent's business enterprise. For example, dad farms sonny boy out to a comparable organization. The understanding is that the kid will learn the ropes and then dump his employer to join up with dear old dad. It's been done often enough, to be sure; but I personally believe such a maneuver is intellectually dishonest. You're buying experience on the cheap, rather than investing in it yourself.

Another seed of destruction can lie in a child's acquiescing to a parent's wish that he extend the family's name by joining the company—but the kid really wants to do something (almost anything!) else. In my own case, I literally grew up in my father's business, as did my eight brothers and sisters. My mother died when the eldest child was 15 years old. It was during the Great Depression, and dad didn't give a thought to splitting us up. So we all had to work to keep the family together. And we kept at it until we could fly on our own. I had no more desire to follow in my dad's footsteps at the family business than I wanted to shoot myself in both feet. Yet none of us would have traded that experience for anything in the world.

Nevertheless, and despite the exceptions I noted, I remain highly skeptical about bringing children and other relatives into a family enterprise. There are too many real hazards for everybody concerned.

PART TWO

Savage
Answers

M any who read my last book, *High Touch Selling,* have written or told me that they felt its most popular chapter is the one concerning the question-and-answer session I had with various insurance agents and/or financial planners.

So, on the strength of that positive reaction, I invited a number of sales professionals to fire away at me with any questions they may have about my methods of operation and anything related to them. I tried to get a solid, representative cross-section.

Here are the names of the participants:

> Dick Balhoff, Connecticut Mutual
> John Ross, independent agent
> Dave Walbom, State Farm
> Mark Smith, Savage Financial
> Wayne Crowther, Northwestern Mutual
> Tim Condon, Savage Financial
> Tom Snow, Scheib & Co.
> Don Thompson, Savage Financial
> Jim Harris, MD, PhD (observer)
> Mark Smigelski, Savage Financial
> Bill Harris, Asset Dynamics
> Phil Jackson, Columbus Life

I supplemented the material from this special discussion with questions I received at the annual Savage Seminar conducted in September 1992 in Toledo, Ohio. Sixty insurance agents from across the country attended, with annual incomes averaging $130,000.

14

Answers on Selling and Success

Question: *John, if you were just starting in the business today, what would you do?*

Savage: I would start with people I knew, with friends—then, from them, build on referrals. I'd never make a cold call. I've never written a direct mail letter; I think that's foolish. Friends, then their referrals, and so on. It's a beautiful way to build a clientele.

Question: *What does it take for a new agent to become a success in this business, in your opinion?*

Savage: Complete dedication to work. Honest effort is always rewarded. Have a good relationship with Almighty God—and that should be your only dependency. If business is down, wait a little bit; it'll get good. If business is real good right off the bat, wait a little bit; it'll get bad. That's the way it goes, ups and downs.

Question: *What are your recommendations for getting the ChFC and the CLU designations?*

Savage: My recommendation is strong for education. I think it's good to get a CLU and a ChFC, if that's what you want to do. In our

---

*In our office I always say we have more
degrees than a thermometer, but we
don't have as much knowledge as I
would like.*

---

office I alawys say we have more degrees than a thermometer, but we don't have as much knowledge as I would like. See, when you get a degree, that isn't the end. Frank Jacobs said he does more studying now than he did in law school—just to keep up. Fine, get the degrees; what that does is open up the opportunity for you to continue to study. What we know today will be history 20 years from now. Continuing education is extremely important—and reading and subscribing to the people who can give you the information.

Question: What subscriptions do you read regularly?

Savage: I don't read anything regularly. I subscribe to 31 different services. I probably don't read 10 percent of everything I subscribe to. What I do is scan, and if I see an interesting article, then I usually call Frank (Jacobs) and say "Frank, what about this article?" He gives it back to me chapter and verse. He might say, "John, the guy doesn't know what he's talking about." Frank tells me 75 percent of all published articles are in error. You've got to be very careful.

Question: What do you think had the most impact on your career development?

Savage: I had a lot of people influence my life—especially Monsignor Jerome Schmitt. In case you haven't heard the story, I was playing basketball seven days a week when I was 25 years of age. I'd go down to the Catholic Club and work out. One day Monsignor Schmitt called me into his office and told me, flat out, that I was the most selfish person he'd ever met in his life. Coming from a man I greatly admired and loved, that blast really hit me. You know, he'd met a whole lot of people. And if I was the worst . . . So I asked him what I could do about it. He said I could stop playing basketball all the time and contribute something as a citizen; spend more time with other people, helping them I followed his advice, immediately Because everything he said was right

Question: *John, I've heard you speak a number of times, and you've often stated that a person should fall in love with himself. In light of what the Monsignor told you, would you expand on that?*

Savage: They're not even in the same context. I think you must fall in love with yourself. That's Christian; that's Christ's teachings. Love your neighbor as yourself—*as yourself.* I think if you fall in love with yourself, you never put yourself above another human being. You're a gift from God, and I think you should be pretty pleased with that. That has nothing to do with disregarding everybody else. Just the opposite. An *I* for an *I* with a capital *I* is not good.

Question: *Who are the people you admire in the industry and what are the reasons for your admiration of them?*

Savage: There are many. I admire Tom Wolff, who's given so much time and energy to develop a successful system to help agents. Ben Feldman and Lau Blessman got me, as a young person in the Roundtable, to think big. Norm Levine has given a lot of energy to the industry. I spent a week in England with the author of *The One Card System,* Hal Granham—very competent, honest and considerate. His system and mine are miles apart; that doesn't make it wrong or right, just different. Dave Hilton, over in Chicago, is a fine, quality person. I respect him totally. And he has a son in the business who's excelling; that I admire. Locally, Bruce Shaw is an extraordinary worker and an amazing guy—as neat and well-groomed after a rough day as he is when he starts out in the morning. But I want to tell you, I don't work as hard as those gentlemen. My personality isn't built for what they undertake. I don't work weeknights, Saturdays and Sundays. I take a lot of time off. I'd rather be at a ball game than on an interview, especially with my kids.

Question: *Has it ever crossed your mind, the wish that you had worked harder, become even more successful?*

Savage: I guess I don't care much for the word successful. Mother Theresa doesn't make a lot of money, OK? No, I can tell you that never occurred to me . . . making more money. I know *that* God has blessed me ten times over ten. I work hard when I work, play hard when I play. But the idea of making more than I've made just never popped into my head.

The caller reluctance, now that was an obstacle.

Question: What are the greatest obstacles you've overcome in your personal and business life?

Savage: That's quite a huge question. Obstacles? I had the most caller reluctance of anyone I knew. I failed for a period of about nine years, coming into the business. The first four years I had dedicated myself to pleasure; I was playing ball all the time. I went back to my high school as a basketball coach, teaching in the afternoons, but still maintaining my insurance business. It was at age 29 that I got married, quit coaching, quit teaching, quit playing games like golf and basketball, and dedicated my life to having a beautiful marriage and great family and just working. I can tell you, there have been no obstacles since I've been married, and we have nine children—even when I was laid up in bed for seven months, at age 35, following surgery; three months in the hospital, then bedridden four months at home, with my wife carrying our fifth child. Some pain, sure, but not what I'd consider an obstacle. The caller reluctance, now *that* was an obstacle. There was no obstacle worth mentioning in my personal life that I can remember.

Question: How did you solve the caller reluctance, then?

Savage: By not having nay. By designing things that people could only say yes to. I don't believe in overcoming objections. I've never bought all that stuff. I just believe that the product is a good product. I started doing total financial planning 30 years ago. I designed all my "circles" to avoid caller reluctance, build a clientele and, I hoped, operate in a professional manner for the benefit of the client.

Question: When you talk about struggling for nine years, was there a turning point?

Savage: I'd say getting married, although my production had been creeping up. I made $5,000, including renewals, in my eighth year. But, let's face it, I didn't really work. I had about one appointment a night, after playing golf all day long, sleeping late   sort of a nice single life

Question: *John, you say you never made a cold call. So, during the time you were struggling, you were working based on referrals then too?*

Savage: Friends and referrals, yes; people I met through sports and elsewhere. But then I got married, and we were living in a little apartment over a store with three children (the eldest was not two years of age). Then we moved out of there into our first home, and I tell you, I just worked hard. I had dinner every night at home and centered my life around my family.

Question: *John, I've known you a long time. What would you say is responsible for your huge success? What are the elements to that? I know you're a hard worker—what else? Your technique? Your approach?*

Savage: I think it has an awful lot to do with that. Going into the "circle" design—total financial planning—was the catalyst for big amounts of business. And then, my approach in the business insurance market is to work with a person sometimes as long as two years without bringing up or doing any business with him or her—just trying to help where I felt I could help with the skills God gave me: ability to communicate. *And,* you get referrals from satisfied customers. I've never bought anything that was canned. When I first started in the business and heard these "approaches"—"Get on the other end and we'll phone each other and pretend"—well, I don't have any pretend bones in my body, and that one just didn't pass the smell test. I'm not an iconoclast (although some would consider me that). I just think we have made things very difficult trying to make a sale, when if we got right to the point we'd be so much better off. I never socialized with prospects. I haven't been a "social" salesman, although I think I'm a social person. That's a tough question, though. This is my 42nd year; things just gradually grow. I'm starting to wonder whether divine intervention doesn't enter my life. I've had a spectacular year this year—and a lot less work.

Question: *I know you started out as a teacher and that you like teaching. As you talk to people, I know you educate and teach them—a different approach, by the way—but do you think that's been important to your success?*

People don't buy insurance; people buy people.

Savage: That's a good question. I think I teach the ideas. I don't think you educate people; you *sell* people. You give them something they can easily digest. I think that when you go out with a proposal, you really are confusing people. Savings is what I totally believe in. When I got married, I had $180 to my name. I'm not proud of that. I made a fair amount of money when I was single, but I never kept score. I'd pick up the tab more often than not. It was at a time when, if one guy had a buck, everybody had a buck. So I never was hung up on dollars. I'm really overpaid today, and I want to give most of it away. My love for making money now is so that more of it can be given away to my many charities. Today, the charity demands on the pocketbook are unbelievable.

Question: *When you're working with business prospects for the first two years without making any sales, what types of things are you making recommendations on?*
Savage: In business insurance (which gives you your quantum leap of bigger cases) I would design circles, make a picture on my board, always in my office. (I had 168 appointments in January, in my office.) When I woke up one day at home, after having been hospitalized so long, I found out that people would come to my bedroom for their annual reviews. I said, "Wow, when I get out of here, we're going to have those reviews in my office. Business insurance is no different from individual insurance. Business insurance is people. People don't buy insurance; people buy people. So you have to build a relationship; then you build a clientele.

Question: *John, as an agent in the business, what do you say is the biggest challenge facing our industry?*
Savage: I think it's a beautiful business, for me. But it's just another business. I really can't change what's happening down the road, nor will I be accountable if the industry folds. How long have you been in the business? Sixteen years? You have no problems. You already have a clientele. Your clientele will take care of you. If you leave and start selling cars, they will buy cars from you. They really

will, once they trust you—and trust is all we have. Once that is violated, we have nothing.

Question: The candor that you seem to show at all times I've seen you—have you always had that in your interviews from the very beginning? Do you always tell people, "This is your problem, this is what you need to do"—a very open approach?

Savage: I think I've been pretty candid all my life. I have never been one to shy away from an answer. Nor have I spent much time in preparing. I have a strong Christian philosophy. I believe I'm serving God by serving man. I don't try to affect people in the wrong way. I'm sure we've all made a lot of mistakes.

Question: What about the force used in getting your points across? How far do your take the people if they don't tend to view things the way you do? Do you just say, well, there's other fish in the sea, or do you really take it to the wall, so to speak?

Savage: In an interview, I never raise my voice. When you're giving a speech, that's a whole different story; you're trying to motivate or teach a group. But when you're one on one with somebody, I think it's a simple conversation. I think "no" is an answer. I don't believe in overcoming objections. I believe in not getting them. I think that if you communicate effectively for the benefit of the buyer, in a systematic methodology, then I think your results are going to be pretty good. Usually, at breakfast, when I first meet a person, is when he or she dismisses me—or vice versa.

Question: How do you handle questions concerning instability in the industry?

Savage: I've been asked probably six times so far this year about the stability of my company. This will happen more to a younger agent, I'm sure. I think it's a matter of concern to you, but you can't worry about it. Let's face it, we'll all go under sometime. It's a question of when. Nothing lasts forever—which is what keeps me light on such a subject. And remember, never attack another company. You never strengthen the weak by weakening the strong. When you start comparing companies and products, you've gotten caught up in how most people were trained in sales—poorly. Sell yourself. You have to do your work. You have to check things out. But you have to have trust, too. Granted, there are a couple of companies now where you can't get your cash values or your dividends. The only thing they're paying are death benefits. That would really bother me. In that kind of a fix, I'd need all the supernatural help I could conjure up. And we don't know who the next one will be. But I'll say this for our industry: We have very few thieves in the administration and home offices of our companies. Of all financial institutions, ours at the home office level will rate far and away number one. I don't think we have any Boeskys. We have a lot of fine people. If we have a total depression, can I tell you what's going to happen to your company? It's going under. If we have a total collapse, it's not the end of the world, is it? Let's get ready for the next one. Treat yourself a little lighter. Don't carry it to bed with you.

Question: In this industry, maybe one of the black marks is the fact that approximately 95 percent of the people who come into it are flushed out in the first two years. You've had a successful agency, a lot of people who are "stayers." Do you attribute that to training, to prescreening, a combination of both?

Savage: I think people don't spend enough time with people. I may be training someone, not see him for perhaps a month, then spend three or four days in a row with him. The instant training is pretty good in our business. But after six months they say goodbye and forget you. People around here will tell you I never forget you, even if you've been around here 20 years. Selection, of course, is important. I had some basic, simple rules: If you run around on your wife, you're fired. I just can't stomach that. I happen to think women are better than men. The ladies in our organization are a big part; the family unit is a strong part. Seventeen years ago I gave three-quarters of the agency to the people— no charge. I sold the quarter I had left at age 60. I've not attended a business management meeting in this organization in 17 years, when I gave up the management role—I stayed out of that camp and let the other person grow. Incidentally, staying out of the other guy's zone is something that doesn't happen too regularly. I got a lot of credit—and discredit—for things I did or did not do; that's part of leadership. Brickbats or praise, neither amounts to much in the final analysis.

Question: How do you motivate people in the industry who are leveling off?

Savage: It's an attitudinal thing, usually. I don't want to preach, and some of the people in the agency are probably sick of hearing me

Don't promise an orchard for an apple, which is what's happening all too often.

repeat this line, but if you don't have your spiritual life and your family life straight, you're gonna have attitude problems sneak up and bite you continually. I rushed home tonight, hugged my wife, sat down and had dinner. I think that's the big thrill of the day. And to see my son come in, finished with his first year of college. He wanted to spend some time with us. That's really the payment for working. But I love my work; thoroughly enjoy it—and teaching. Locally, I guess I'm getting a little tired of hearing myself talk to groups. I had ten speaking engagements in the past seven days, because I said yes in February.

Question: Have you had any spiritual experiences along the way that affected your life?
Savage: I've never had a dream or vision. Nothing that I could "put my hands on." Yet I feel good all the time. I consider that a gift. I'm a pretty tranquil person. I believe in God and am happy in my religion. I got great direction from my father, who raised nine kids without a mate. I don't want to get into this too much, but there is a cloud of paganism in this country so deep you can hardly see through it. That will change.

Question: How do you define your natural market? Do you believe in such a thing as a natural market?
Savage: Every living, breathing human being is a prospect. That's the natural market. I think we get all caught up in "the medical market," or "the business market." Everybody's a market. But be careful. Don't promise an orchard for an apple, which is what's happening all too often. About 20 years ago, we in the industry were told that we had to compete against the Merrill Lynches and the Kidder Peabodys and companies like that. I have never, ever understood that—why we should start selling our product as an investment when it never was and never will be an investment. And then we said we had to get into the investment business. Well, I think you can do a lot of money management without selling those other vehicles, which is what

I've chosen to do. Care and work—and when you're young, you have to work awfully hard.

Question: John, you say your closing ratio is close to 100 percent, that it's been high for years. . .

Savage: One hundred percent now, high for the past 20 years. But that means 20 years when it wasn't high. There were many times when I came away from interviews really disappointed that I didn't make the sale.

Question: In the last 20 years, was it just confidence that closed that many? Where's the difference in the rest of us not getting that high a percentage?

Savage: Let me say, the training in this business is terrible . . . terrible! But I've found it's not too good anywhere. The basic training and teaching of every facet of sales, I think, misses the boat. I sit in meetings and can't believe what I hear, or what I read about what's being taught. "If they say no, that doesn't mean no." If no doesn't mean no, what does it mean? We're caught up in so many misconceptions of what a sale is. "Tell 'em anything as long as they buy." "Have your pencil ready; get the check." Like it's trickery. All those things I heard I couldn't stomach. I attended my first convention in 1957 and earned half my way. I drove a car back for a dealership and they paid me $50, and they paid for the gas. I learned how to cut down expenses real quick. On that trip, the president of the company said I took life too lightly and would never make it.

Question: What are the elements that go into a successful closing?

Savage: In closing, there are none. In my life, it's how are your openings? If people like you, they buy from you. If they don't buy from you, they didn't like you. Hate to tell you that. Of course, management has said if they turn you down, don't take it personally. Great statement; in other words, if you were turned down, it wasn't because of you but because of what you were selling. Wrong. Totally wrong. People don't "buy" companies. When we started our little agency, we weren't even heard of, a dot on the map. Aetna had the largest agency in the United States, in Toledo, Ohio, and it was the third-largest company. Aetna doesn't have an office today. What makes an agency are the *people* in the agency. Agencies don't get rid of bums. What we have to do is start selecting really well, then train really well, then spend a whole lot of time with the agents. But there are no closes, no closes; they take that away from you. Yet there are books written and videotapes produced on closes, and there's a lot of money being made on both. Beware of them.

Question: You work a lot by referral. How do you get them?

Savage: I work *totally* by referral. I get them by asking my clients for them. You get lazy as you get older, when you make a lot of sales. Still, I'm the only one in our agency who sees every one of his clients every year. Most of those people I saw in January will never buy again, and they still come in. But reviews keep you excited about life and effective in your selling. It's like hitting tee shots; you'll do better if you do it more often than anybody else.

Question: You talk about building client relationships, and I would like to find out your opinion of using a newsletter for a contact vehicle.

Savage: I think newsletters are very good, especially if they're newsworthy, and especially if the people like to get and read them. So that takes you down to about 3 percent of all the letters you send out. And those are the people who know you well. I think it's better to visit people and spend time with them. But are you comfortable with a newsletter? If so, you should continue to do it, because some people do well with newsletters and a lot of their clients like to get them. You know, I go to the mailbox, and do you know what my goal is? Nothing is there. We get so much junk mail ("You have hit the jackpot!").

Question: I'd like you to talk about how you started to take the three months off. Did you just jump right into that? All of a sudden one year you said, by golly that's an idea—or did you take four weeks and then six weeks? And if you take three, why not six?

Savage: Fine, that's asked often and that's a great question. When I was a young man, I dedicated my life to pleasure until I got married at 29. Then I really worked hard. I put all my energy into going to work. Two years later I had two children. Two years after that I had four children, and the oldest one was three years of age. I decided at that time to take one month off, December. I took the kids sledding— spent a lot of time with them. When my oldest guy was in the sixth grade, I announced that I was going to give up the general agency when he went to high school. I knew I couldn't run the agency and be at all the ball games. The kids were deep into athletics, a very enjoyable thing. It was important to spend time with them. So, as long as I was giving up the agency (which was 17 years ago), I might as well increase my time off from one month to three months. That's how I started my three-month vacations. I just don't go to the office. In fact, Wilma just called here and I had my daughter take the call. I simply don't like phone calls when I'm off work. You work enough; you should get balance in your life. For me, it's worked out marvelously well. This seminar is the only thing I'm doing in four months that even looks like work. October 1 I suit up again.

Question: *You mentioned that the One-Card System is a poor way to prospecting—using a see ten, see three, sell one, versus just putting relationships in referrals. Don't you use the One-Card System as a follow-up or organizational tool?*

Savage: If you're going to quote me, it's important that you quote me accurately. I believe my system is better than a One-Card System. I'm not against the latter; I'm against me using it. I'm not against drinking. Come over to our house, you'll get a drink. I just prefer not to. I say, if you take a yellow pad—which I use all the time—and put a list of the people you are going to see for that 30-day period, and then see the names scratched off, now it's like a race. You feel good when you only have to see three more people. Some people would rather work than play. I say anybody who would rather work than play has never played. Play is more fun than work. But workaholics get caught up and they have to go seven days a week. And what happens to them? They die, just like the ones who weren't workaholics. Might as well have a few good times along the way. I think the One-Card System sort of gives me too much organizational work. I like to be looser than that. At the start of a year, I know I'm going to see all my clients; at least, they are all going to be asked in. These are my goals, this is how I'm going to do it. And I'm not married to a system. I think you can get systematized right out the window.

Question: *John, you said you didn't use the One-Card System. Which one do you use?*

Savage: I use the no-card system. I have the board; that's all I use. My three-circles sales presentation is a fact-finder, total financial planning, everything built into one sheet of paper.

Question: *What about your method of follow-up for reviews?*

Savage: I call my secretary in; she fills out the applications and sets up appointments for the reviews. It's all taken care of right then and there with the clients. Then the secretary takes down the pertinent summary information I give her from the board—seven short line entries—and puts it in their file. No more dictations, no mechanical equipment at all.

Question: *The people you're going to be seeing just once a year for annual reviews—do you try to go through those as quickly as you can over a two or three-month period, or do you do so many each month, or does it depend on the year?*

Savage: I try to get it all done in three months—January, May and September. January is my biggest month. We called 213 people to come into the office for that month; 168 showed up. You'll find that fall-off from time to time. The older the client, the less you see of them. The people who've been my clients going back 25 years, they come to the office at 79 percent a year; only 21 percent slippage there. I have nearly 1,000 clients and 880 live in Toledo. I have 80 people I don't see at all. There's no reason to see them. I see them at a rate of about 200 a month. This year I was off four months. Next year it'll be five months.

Question: *Do you try to coordinate reviews with policy anniversaries?*

Savage: No. I've never correlated with policy anniversary. I used to do that. But pretty soon people who can't come in January come in in February. It's by people; we just try to get the people in.

Question: *Let's go back to the three circles. How do you get people who've never been savers to change their spots and want to build a financial plan?*

Savage: I don't think you get a lot of people to change. We're all creatures of habit. But if you get them young enough, it's a fresh breath of air, easier to do. Incidentally, do you know how many people want to fill out sheets? Nobody. Start with that. You have to simplify. That's why I go to the three circles all the time; to make it simple.

Question: The rating services—all the changes—are confusing for people in the business. It leaves the consumer totally in the dark. Do you think there's going to be a central rating service, or will there be a burst of new companies wanting insurance companies to pay them $25,000 just to rate them?

Savage: You said it all in a nutshell. It's a business. We have more new rating companies this year than we had in the last two years. And an insurance company gives them a check for $25,000 and says "We'd like a nice rating." And they all get a nice rating. I remember Standard & Poor's—there were only 18 AAA rated companies. Now it's 50. People say, "Hey, you didn't rate us triple-A; here's our story." How long before the buying public will be kept out of the dark? Forever. That's why your integrity is so important. There's no way the buying public can keep up today with what's going on. Everything they get is prejudiced. Editorial page? Every page is an editorial page, depending on the stories' authors. People say to me, "John, give me an objective opinion." Well, the word *opinion* means subjective.

Question: Do you mail out something like an estate plan or anything else before an annual review?

Savage: No. I do no mailings, except the policy. Don't do anything if you don't have to do it. Remember my theme: Many, many people are doing things very, very well that they shouldn't even be doing, because it makes them feel good. You know how many people sit behind a mechanical piece of equipment three hours a day? A computer? It's a game. It's Itari moved to the office. They just enjoy working with the numbers. And you know the company has done all the work. It's all actuarily the same.

Question: John, to continue on with your review process, when it comes time to determine the need for life insurance and the premium, what do you have prepared before your client comes in?

Savage: Nothing. I bake the cake from scratch. Did you ever eat a cake baked from scratch, or eat a cake that was in the box? Know the difference? What my wife cooks and I eat, and what they're eating across this country—I would throw up. That's the difference. I think you have to individualize everybody. When you start pulling something

I think salespeople have a terrible, terrible reputation—well deserved.

off the shelf and say, "This was made just for you," you're talking to yourself. Because these people didn't come in on a turnip truck.

Question: What's your philosophy behind mailing the policies? That goes against all insurance philosophy—I mean, sale is made at delivery, deliver your policies, develop the relationship . . .

Savage: My philosophy—well, I hope I go against what's going on. If I'm going *with* somebody, I'm really bothered by that. When I came into the business, they said, "Deliver the policy, because it's been six weeks since it's been issued and they'll have forgotten what they bought." I would say to myself, I'll go out and explain it and six weeks later they will forget again. If they're forgetful people, they're going to forget. Guys, I've done all the hard work. I did 26-page proposals on estate planning when I was 28 years old. I'd go out and see the people two or three years later, and they couldn't find it. And when they did, dust—it never was opened. I say there's a difference between reality and what other people think. Where am I getting my guidance? From home office people who aren't in the game. I contend that if you tell your people you're looking forward to their annual review, you then get another nice visit with them, and it's not a trick to get into the house by delivering the policy. You put it on a professional basis. I think salespeople have a terrible, terrible reputation—well deserved. It's why I'm spending so much time trying to change that. I think selling has a tremendous future. But our colleges haven't found out yet. The dentist doesn't send you anything. He fills your tooth. Does he come out to your house a month later and say, "How's that coming?" No, he says "You will be back in six months." You think you're a salesperson? Check the dentist. How many people here have kids? I learned more about selling from the dentist. He takes you in a dark room and says, "Your kid's teeth are coming out a little bit. Need braces, or else this is what you kid's going to look like (you have fangs, boy). You want you kid to look like this when he goes to high school?" And Kate says, "Certainly not; put those braces on right now." And I went, ho hum, just saw another one. Folks, does the dentist educate you on the anatomy of the mouth? No—just drills. People say they can't get people to come to their office. The dentist does. Those people are out there waiting to be hurt. *We* don't hurt anybody. Please, pay attention to what's going on around you. Be professional. All your client wants you to do is serve and be honest. Like the story about this attorney who screwed up. The client went to him and said, "Hey, I just talked to this other guy and this is really screwed up." He says, "You're right, I made a mistake, I'm sorry, let's see what we can do." And the guy never sued him. The trouble is, a lot of people just say, "That's tough, buddy. Kiss off." Then they get marched in to court. And I think that's where the doctors fail; if they had better bedside relationships, they wouldn't get so many malpractice suits.

Question: Spend a little more time with us on specifically what you say after you have developed a relationship, but you've not gotten referrals from this person. He's one of your top 50, and he's never referred you.

Savage: First, you should be on a mission of referrals. You can't mix the two. I don't think you can both sell and get referrals. They're two different thought processes. I think you have to take a satisfied client to breakfast, at which time you tell him how important it is—if he is happy—to pass the word on. Some people use accountants, some use attorneys to refer a lot of people to them. I've never found it comfortable to do that. But I have found that businesspeople will send you to other businesspeople. You know, "birds of a feather flock together." You will not see these corporate guys—in our community— ever with an entrepreneur. They all hang together and the entrepreneurs hang together. I find it comfortable taking them to breakfast, asking them who they know and would be in a comfortable position to refer me to. Now, what I exactly say—and I think this is where we make a mistake—you've got to say it your way. You've got to use your personality. I don't think there is terminology to pass on. What I say to someone and what you say to someone is going to be different. Satisfied people will pass you on.

Question: John, I'm thinking of the young guy who's reading this book about you having all your appointments in your office. Obviously, it's a nice goal for the young person, along with annual reviews, and when he asks for referrals, he gets ten names thrown at him. But that wasn't always the case for you, though, or was it?

Savage: I've never gotten ten names from anybody. I've never asked for more than one referral at a time. It's not a lottery situation, it's a personal relationship. I would never call someone if somebody hadn't called that person first. Back to the important point you brought up: Everybody in this room should strive to have every appointment in the office—starting at age 21, by the way, not as a long-range goal. We talk about professionalism, but we don't do it very well. The dentist does not come to your home. The doctor did not quit making house calls because he didn't like going to your home. He couldn't take care of the many people who needed his services. It has nothing to do with making money. He had to serve more people; he could do that if they came in. This may come as a surprise to you: Your client would rather come in!

Question: John, I want to know if you have any tips with regard to those of us who go to the client's home. How do we make the transition and start them coming to the office?

Savage: How many clients do you have now? About 300? My guess is that you can move 150 maximum to come in to see you. But everybody new you get, make sure you bring them in. Pretty soon you're going to have 850 over here, and you're going to have 150 there. When I established 25 years ago that I had to build a big clientele, I couldn't do it going to homes. I had the same problem. There are people, first of all, who won't come in. Or, an old friend/client type comes in and just wants to talk about basketball. He'll say, "I don't need any insurance, right, John?" And I'll agree. See, if he says he doesn't need any, there's only one thing to say: "You're right." So, you've established a relationship of going out; continue to go out.

Question: In bringing clients into the office under the context of offering total financial planning, do you think there is a benefit or possibly a disadvantage to being in an agency? Looking down the road, do you think I'd do better to take my own space, to create some separation, so it doesn't look like I'm nothing more than simply a representative of one company, rather than that I'm out there trying to protect the client?

In a business case, I believe you should only talk to the president of a company.

Savage: I think you're always going to protect your client, no matter where you are. And believe me, they're not even thinking the way you're thinking. They're going to buy from you. You are the relationship, not the company. If the company goes under, find out how important that is to them. They aren't going to call the company for their money. They're going to call you. They're going to buy you. Wherever you're comfortable, they're going to be comfortable.

Question: *If a company has a good track record, whether it be your company or another one—if they're financially solvent now, and you've done your research, can you be pretty safe that they're going to be around in 30 years?*
Savage: No. You can do all the homework in the world and you cannot predict 30 years out. There'd be some companies you'd be pretty sure are going to be here. Coca Cola. But you wouldn't want to bet everything you've got that 30 years from now Coca Cola is going to be here. Imagine: They hired an expert and the first thing he did was to change the syrup. Here's something that's lasted for 112 years, and the guy says, "The syrup can be improved." And they probably paid him a lot of money. How long did that last? There was public outcry. They were so smart: "You can have the classic or the bad stuff," I guess. They never named it, you know. That was quick on their part. But you get used to things.

Question: *Of your many family clients, what percentage have both spouses come in for an appointment, as opposed to only one?*
Savage: With the younger people, the husband and wife come in. And that will more than likely continue. But as soon as you move into business insurance, the wife will rarely ever come in, except for the doctor. In those cases, most of the time, the husband and wife will come in. It's an interesting study. Lawyers, no. Accountants, no. I don't understand why; I never had a course in psychology.

Question: Let's say you were referred to Mr. Businessman, and you meet him. Tell us how you conceptually go about the appointment.

Savage: I think you approach each person differently. In a business case, I believe you should only talk to the president of a company. It takes a lot of thought on how to approach that person comfortably for both people. Take The Andersons. I was involved with that company for five years and never brought up what I did—maybe 100 or more meetings, and never, ever tried to sell my product. *[Questioner: Strictly social, you mean?]* No, no; I'd go to help them where they needed help. That's always been my approach to the bigger client. Then they want to pay me for non-insurance-type assistance. My stock answer is that someday you'll need what I have, you'll do business with me, and then I get paid very well. Someday. Funny, but that frustrates some of my business contacts. It gets to a point where they're asking what they can do for me. It's called patience. The race of life is never won by the swift but by the sure. Don't be in a hurry. That's what management misses in this business: "You gotta get your goals. If you don't have ten cases by next month, you're no longer gonna be in this organization. We are winners here." I just get so fed up with all that stuff. I don't think there are any broad guidelines that can work with prospects in general. Nor can any philosophy, unless you buy it inside first.

Question: There's got to be a point in the process, though, when you say, this is something you want to do. The close, the moment of truth that you bring up, or you wait for them to bring up. . . .

Savage: It works both ways. Coincidentally, Dick Anderson (CEO of The Andersons), during a car ride, said, "John, one thing I'll never understand is how you make a living." I've sold him, but he doesn't understand how I'm always free when it comes to non-insurance assistance. So, guys, I haven't made a written proposal to anybody in 25 years. The dentist doesn't educate you in the anatomy of the mouth. You don't shop around for a cut-rate surgeon. You select the doctor. It's a matter of trust. And you never ask the price. For surgery? You want the lowest? The guy who's the resident? Ain't nobody in the bargain guy's office. Let me add that I think we kill ourselves in our approach. People sense the person in a hurry. They resent doing business with an agent who is pressing. Maybe it's partly due to golf. Supposedly, golf is for recreation, to relieve stress. But I get the

---

Businesspeople do not want to make a career out of a meeting.

---

impression the game more often causes tension. I see guys get all bent out of shape, throwing clubs and balls in the air, then setting a date for 7 o'clock the next morning so they can resume the torture. Or they play ten times a year, and they blame the game. I used to play a lot, but I'll tell you that if I went and played tomorrow, I couldn't break 100.

Question: *To get back to the breakfast appointment, where you conduct an awful lot of your business. . .*

Savage: I have a breakfast appointment every morning, all through referrals. Number one: mental rehearsal, on the way to the appointment; very important. Plan—to listen to the prospect! We're going to talk and I'm not going to try to sell. And I'm going to try to get them to come into my office. That's my whole approach. The dialogue goes something like this, with me saying, "Jim, Harry thought it would be good for you and me to just get together and meet each other. He seemed to be happy with some of the things I've done for him. Be assured that if after this breakfast you see no merit whatsoever, then we'll part ways, say goodbye and have a pleasant day. But if sometime during this breakfast there's something that you feel I can help you with, bring it up and I'll be the first to tell you." Casual. Comfortable. Again, these are usually solid referrals. You'll get 90 percent of them from 10 percent of your clientele. I have one fellow who's sent me 60 people if he's sent me one.

Question: *You say you don't write up proposals. But what if you get a prospect who wants one?*

Savage: It never comes up. When people say to me they would like to see something, they just don't. Notice my method. When I come into my office, I go to the board. And I explain to them that we're going to keep this very simple. Now, when I put it on the board I always ask, "Have you ever seen anything so simple that tells the whole story?" They all say "No, I really like this." You see, the beauty of drawing the circles on the board is that you're individualizing every prospect, as opposed to a proposal that's printed and organized ahead of time It works the same for the business prospect. Only remember what a businessman told me 30 years ago: "John, talk to me in short sentences." Businesspeople do not want to make a career out of a meeting. They're interested in their business; if you can help them, fine. But don't waste their time or use language they have trouble following.

Question: Aside from your business activities, do you have any other projects or goals you haven't done yet but that you want to do?

Savage: Oh, yes. Your question is very timely. I've worked in the Toledo Catholic Diocese's Central City Ministry for 20 years. It's where I grew up. And I've had a lot of fun helping Monsignor (Martin) Donnelly in the Ministry's youth program, which serves several inner-city schools. I have a year and a half to go with this effort before I'm finished. Then I'm going to swing over to work at an inner-city public school. I'll be there every day. I just think there's not enough courage in the inner cities—not enough people commanding respect. Yet I think you can have the same discipline in the public schools as you have in the parochial or other private schools. I want to give it a go. God may spin me out of here before I get to it, but it remains my burning goal at the moment. You see, if we don't change the central city structure in this country, it's all over. If you think today's kids are undisciplined, wait until the next bunch comes flying through. Nobody's doing much about it. It's like ice on the Titanic; have another drink, not knowing that they're going down. Our major cities are really shaky. Thinking "it" will go away. It's not going to go away. There's got to be responsibility at every level.

Question: How has your community involvement helped your business?

Savage: If you were to ask ten people in town about my community involvements, you'd get ten different answers. I'm not myopic enough to believe those activities have not helped me in some way or another, from a business standpoint. On the other hand, I've always made it a firm rule never to make a proposal to anyone on any board on which I've served, or to the institutions involved. And I've been on a lot of boards, including those of four colleges. I was on the University of Toledo board nine years. Never once did I talk with anyone there about business. My second year on that board, they brought some business to me. I declined, saying I'd never do that while on the board, or after I left it. Conversely, I brought seven of my clients to the board of the University of Toledo's corporation—a private, supportive body. Nor have I ever made a business approach to any of the other 19 members of the university's corporation. Sure, there's an advantage in meeting and working with people. And it's bound to generate business; I didn't just fall off a tomato truck. But it's really hard to pin down where things may have developed—which came first, the chicken or the egg? That's as close as I can come to an honest answer.

The other side of the coin is the often humorous perception some people have of me. For example, when Magic Johnson got ill, I got a phone call from one of the local TV stations: "John, we understand you have Magic's insurance." I told him it wasn't true. Then, "Well, we know you work with Isiah Thomas." To which I said, "Let me help you before this goes too far along. If I were you, I'd be calling Isiah Thomas, or Magic." I don't think it's my job to reveal my clientele to the western world. The stories really get farfetched. A classic evolved from a trip I'd taken to Medjugorje, Yugoslavia, where six children have claimed to see visions of the Blessed Virgin Mary. I got a call one day from Lourdes College, asking if I'd introduce a cousin of one of the visionary children prior to her speech. I said that although I'd met the kids, I didn't know the girl, but that I'd be happy to accept the invitation. I gave the intro, heard the speech and then was approached by a reporter from the *Toledo Blade,* who asked me whether I'd had a vision or dream or seen any miracles while in Medjugorje. I said no to each. The next day wife Kate raps on the bathroom door while I'm taking a shower and says, "Wait until you see the Sunday paper!" Front page: "John Savage Goes to Medjugorje." I can say I wasn't misquoted. But it was really a nothing story, made almost out of thin air. I don't understand it from a journalistic point of view. But there I was, featured in a big story, and I was stuck with it. Maybe the moral is don't be surprised at how you're perceived or what the media might say about you.

Question: So many of us have goals to happiness, such as "I'll really be happy when I make the Million Dollar Round Table." You seem to be happy every day. What can you tell us so that we'll enjoy the trip instead of saying we're going to be happy when?

Savage: It's hard to evaluate myself on that score, but old friends say I've always been unflappable and pretty happy-go-lucky. I've never liked anybody beating up on the little guy. I don't like bullies.

From my earliest years, I guess I always had empathy toward people. That helps; just caring. As for being unflappable, I must've come by it from birth.

Question: *How about some overall guidelines—what we should and shouldn't be doing.*

Savage: First, get your personal life straightened out, every day. Examine your conscience. That is a beautiful place to start. Don't read anything you wouldn't give to your children to read. Don't spend an inordinate amount of time at the movies or in front of a television set, because you may end up at the same level mentally. See how many areas you can get involved in where nobody knows you're involved. Be available to help people. Be amiable, nice to be around. Smile and the world smiles with you. Have a keen sense of awareness. Be positive. For the base, have a strong spiritual life. That's like disability income; it'll hold up all the other stuff. An unexamined life isn't worth living; an unexamined thought isn't worth expressing. Master the dictionary and the Bible.

15

Answers on Insurance Products

Question: *I've always been concerned about the use of annuities, and I use a lot of them personally. But the problem I have is that there's no stepped-up basis on the death of the annuitant. You mentioned yesterday that you do a lot of annuities. In terms of overall estate planning, how do you deal with the matter of the stepped-up basis or lack thereof?*

Savage: I don't think you even have to concern yourself. With retirees, I do a lot of annuities. If a person comes to me with $900,000 of liquid estate, I put $300,000 in an annuity, $300,000 in Treasury bills and maybe $300,000 in a tax-free bond. Now, I don't sell, nor do I get a commission for, the bonds or the treasuries. I get paid by the commission. One thing you don't want to do is get overly caught up on any regulation. What you want to get caught up in is that the people have enough money. When you get into big estates—I sold one guy $5 million in an annuity, and he has $50 million of liquid money; so a disproportionate amount is going elsewhere. You have to be very careful selling annuities as the end-all. That's where you make a mistake when you get in the stepped-up basis.

Question: *Are you against using the Economic Circle of Life if you have somebody who doesn't yet have any assets or insurance?*

Savage: I would not use the Economic Circle of Life presentation if people don't have anything. There's nothing to really talk about. There are many simpler forms of the three circles, and things like that, to use. My book *High Touch Selling* contains just about every one of my ideas.

Question: I think I know your philosophy on spending the premium a little more wisely, but what about policies for little kids?
Savage: When a child dies it's an economic gain to a family. They don't have to feed, clothe or educate. That's economics. It has nothing to do with love. I say you buy insurance on your children after you've satisfied the need for protection of husband and wife, in total estate planning. Then get some coverage on the children; give them a jump-start in their protection program. I did that with all of my children. I had $3 million on my life and $1 million on my wife, and all of my children got $100,000 worth of life insurance coverage. They own a lot now. But if you had me as your father, you'd own a lot now, too.

Question: Yesterday, when I said I had the $400,000 and no children and you said I had enough—now, maybe it's my training, but at some point, if I can afford it and it fits with my future plans, would it not be wise to buy more now in anticipation of greater wealth later? To save the money?
Savage: You have no children and you have $400,000 worth of life insurance coverage. From a need standpoint, you probably don't have a big need of protection. That would depend, of course, on the health of your wife, on her income. Nobody ever died and left too much, as far as the widow would go. I'm sure if you had $10 million and you died, there'd be a dance at the casket. But I'm just talking about need versus want. There's nothing wrong with buying some more and then, of course, using it for estate taxes, if that comes into being, or even giving it to charity.

If I die first, a third of the entire estate goes to charity. Those charities have all been named. I have to take care of the wife, because she may live a long time. I would think, when I do die, her situation will be bettered—especially if she picks up another guy. She's a real catch: "How're you fixed for money?" "Well, I got a little here."

Question: John, can you get into the charitable bequest theme a little more in depth for some of us who would like to get more into that market? How do we go about developing the system within our own community? How did you do it?

Savage: First of all you have to have a philosophy. You don't *become* a giver. You're a giver or a taker, really. I think that's all money is good for, to give away. And I think if you're overpaid, as I am, you should give a considerable amount to charity. I think what you look for are people who've had a habit of giving to an organization, whether it be the United Way or a college. Then you approach that person and say, "I notice you've been so good to these schools." That's what I did with Harold McMaster. I introduced him to giving a lot more on a deferred giving, through an insurance contract that cost him pennies on the dollar, so he could give away a lot more at his death than he could ever give with 100 cents on the dollar. He bought that beautifully. In fact, what I sold him—and I wish he were here; there's no secret to this, by the way—was the idea of buying $2 million worth of life insurance: 20 contracts, $100,000 each. And then, when a charity would call him, he would just give them one of the policies. He would pay the premium to that charity, and that charity would then pay it to the insurance company. That way he got to take care of a lot of people—and $100,000 is a lot to a little charity. That appealed to him. I still think it comes back to selling. I don't think you can sell somebody who's never given to anybody on giving $1 million to a university, or even $100,000.

If you're going to work in the charitable area, there's tons written on the charitable remainder trust. Now, charitable remainder trust, in a nutshell, is giving a lump sum to a charity. The income goes to the person who wants to set up the charity. Then, when he or she dies, the lump sum stays with the charity. That sounds good. And everybody is excited about what sounds good. But there aren't many of them established. I like the direct giving of a life insurance contract by a person to a charity. I find that simpler. I have never sold a charitable remainder trust. And I can lecture on it for an hour.

Question: We talked about estate planning and setting up a trust. Can you tell us what your process would be the first time you meet with a client who does not have the trust? Do you establish the need for insurance, then recommend he meet with an attorney and come back to you and buy it?

Savage: The biggest thing I learned in trust work is you can change beneficiaries. You should make the sale to fund the trust before

Every contract is actuarily the same.

the trust is established. Now, we're not talking about an irrevocable trust; we're talking about a simple AB trust. With an irrevocable trust you can't do that, because you've got gift and contemplation of death. So you've got a three-year problem there. But in a regular AB trust, if I'm doing financial planning or estate planning for a person, and he agrees he needs a trust—and the funding of the life insurance is sold—when I make the sale, then we meet with the lawyer. Then all we have to do is change the beneficiary from the individual to the trust itself.

Question: What would be your process in the area of the irrevocable trust?

Savage: Irrevocable trust is a long, drawn-out affair—I would say five or six meetings—and I've sold a number of them. I refer them to Frank Jacobs. But some of my clients have their own lawyers. So, I go to those people. But I have never referred anybody and then had them go sideways on me and bring in another practitioner. That'd take the guts of ten burglars. I don't think there's any worry about you losing anything, because you're bringing something to them and you're going to be the beneficiary of writing that business. But you can't believe how many people get right down to the end and then decide they don't want the insurance that's been recommended. Then, I'd say take half of it now, and half of it maybe a few years from now. Or a quarter of it. That's your judgment in reading what's happening during all these meetings. A lot of time is involved in good estate planning.

Question: I haven't heard you address the need for disability income. Would you do that now?

Savage: I draw my three circles—bank, investment, insurance. Then I draw you. This is your income, which is going to make that all happen. If one gets out of commission, or this balloon busts and you become totally disabled, these will all fall. Now, let's get back to how much disability income I do. Outside of the professional groups, there's not much market anymore, because so many businesspeople, including

You pay more, they pay quicker. You pay less, you pay longer.

entrepreneurs, have good disability programs. Often the guy who writes the group insurance has an individual disability. But the group people don't do much estate planning; they don't have enough time, energy or expertise. I don't sell a lot of disability income, but I have many doctors with disability coverage. However, I'm not getting many new doctors because of my age. So I probably make only about 10–12 disability sales a year.

Question: What is your feeling, John, on the sale of modified endowment contracts for older individuals who are insurable?

Savage: I've never sold a modified endowment contract. That's my feeling. Remember what we said earlier—every contract is actuarily the same. That's what you have to know about an insurance company. You pay more, they pay quicker. You pay less, you pay longer. Every contract's exactly the same, based on mortality and, of course, investment of the company, which is the same for every contract written in the company. Administrative costs are the same.

Question: We've talked about the cash values and companies that are claiming they pay 7 percent or 6 percent or 8 percent, or whatever. Will there be whole life or universal life top contracts in which the guarantees are 4 or 4½ percent? I always try to give my people some sort of ledger so they know what they've bought. And, of course, they're showing the current rates, and I explain to them that at least these are somewhat intrasensitive. Do you not show people what the cash values are? And one other question: One of the markets we use is a mortgage acceleration market, where instead of paying extra on the mortgage, you buy a life insurance contract and use the cash value to pay off the mortgage 15 or 20 years later. That's assuming we're going to get better than 4½ percent interest on the contract. . .

Savage: Well, your question got so long—(*Questioner: How do you feel about paying 7 or 8 percent in today's market?*)

We have tall buildings with nobody in 'em, and insurance companies have the total mortgage.

Savage: If you make a presentation to someone where they'll pay 7 percent on a universal life contract, and you sell minimum amount of dollars going in to fund that contract, and ten years later the market drops to 4 percent, which is happening now, you're going to have an unhappy client. Now, most contracts are sold with a minimum amount of dollars, because you only got full commission on a minimum amount of dollars. The practitioner was more interested in commission than in taking care of the client's needs. I've never funded one like that. I fund my contracts pretty strongly so in case you do get a dip, they're an intrasensitive contract. Personally, I think we're looking at seven or eight more years of low interest, irrespective of who gets into office. I think economics will dictate political moves, instead of the politicians dictating, because we're out of money. We are in bad shape financially in the world, and that's the same with insurance companies.

Question: *But can they pay a 7 or 6 percent interest rate to their policyholders over the next ten years?*
Savage: No. You cannot pay 7 percent for a long period of time if you're earning 4 percent. Without mentioning companies, one that is in the jackpot of the top ten insurance companies in America has 34 percent of its assets in mortgages that were paying 12 and 11 percent return. This one company has 40 percent vacancy in those mortgages. Can I tell you what the vacancies pay? We have tall buildings with nobody in 'em, and insurance companies have the total mortgage. That's what the insurance industry has fallen into. I'll say this from the highest mountain in the land: Savings and loans—most of them went under because of thieves. Banks have fewer thieves, but they have some poor loan situations out there. The insurance industry has no thieves, but it's got a tremendous amount of its portfolio in mortgages, and I'm not talking about junk bonds. And by the way, junk bonds are back! Isn't that great? We are an amazing society. We got rid of one batch of junk bonds—gotta buy all that stuff, the government had to bail

> ***I** say every insurance company that*
> *changes a contract should pay no*
> *commission. That would really increase*
> *people's integrity.*

out—and now we've got those creative guys at the top of the ladder who have no integrity. Understand, they're highly educated, in the great citadels of advanced learning, but they're thieves. And a bright thief is very difficult to catch—until you owe him a billion or so. I grew up with some dumb thieves. Guy from the neighborhood got picked up for robbery nine years ago and just got out recently. I saw his wife here, working at the hotel. I asked her how he's doing. She said he's back in—like, here's a piece of gum. They get caught. They rob the same bank, and they have no mask. Before they get home they're caught. So, while our industry has solid people, if you have bad mortgages, you're still going to have difficulty.

Question: Following up on that, John, can you make a prediction or an analysis of where universal life contracts are going to be in the industry, say, ten years from now?

Savage: I'm not Solomon. I think the universal life contract will be here ten years from now. All you have to do is wait. Right now is a bad time for the universal product, because the interest rates are so low. I hope everybody doesn't sell their universal products and go buy ordinary products. Unethical practitioners might say, "You've got this, now you should have that." Sell, cancel this, and you make another commission. Eight years later it's "Ah, that was good then, but now you better have this." And another commission is paid. I say every insurance company that changes a contract should pay no commission. That would really increase people's integrity. You know, if you had to do something without getting paid, you wouldn't do it long.

Question: You talked about college education being paid for with tax-free income. You said you were going to elaborate on that.

Savage: It's pretty difficult, in a microphone, to describe it, but see if you can follow this sequentially. You take a life insurance contract. It has cash value of $25,000. Then, think of the mortgage on

---

I've been in the business 42 years, and I pay all full premiums every year.

---

their house: They have a $120,000 home with a $40,000 mortgage. Now you come on the scene. They've got a kid 17 years of age, another 15 and another 13. What I do is get a $60,000 mortgage right away and put it in a funnel for education, knowing these three people can get through a state school (and they can do that—they're going to work and things like that) and you're going to be down to zero at the end. Their life insurance continues to increase, and at the end of the rainbow it's $60,000. Well, when we took this money out and put it over here, we increased the payment on the mortgage. And a new mortgage of $100,000 the first nine years is 90 percent interest. Interest is deductible. So you've made college education tax-deductible, and you've paid it back with a tax-free transfer of the cash value back to the mortgage payment.

Question: You were talking about how bad vanishing premiums are for the industry. Conceptually, what is the difference between borrowing money out of your policy that you're not going to pay back until death?

Savage: Now wait a minute. You're not paying attention. We borrowed it out and we paid it back. See, I don't have any trouble with borrowing money, but here's a regular life insurance contract. You borrow the cash value and you pay it back with dividends. I don't think you should ever borrow anything not to pay it back unless it's a small amount. If you borrow a big amount to help a situation, I think you should get that money back in there because you may need it again. There is a difference. In borrowing out, you continue to pay premiums. And premiums are the lifeblood. They have to loan the money out, too, after you give it to them. So, they're loaning it out a 6 percent. It's when you borrow and you don't pay any more that you're a drain on the cash flow of the company. And, by the way, why do you do it? You think it helps you make a sale. It's really interesting.

Do you still pay your premiums for your own life insurance? *"Yes."* How long have you been in the business? *"Thirty-five years."*

Thirty-five years—and then he tells his customer not to pay? If it was better, *he* wouldn't pay. See, that's the old golden rule: Do for your customers what you would have them do for you. How long have you been in the business? *"Eighteen years."* Do you pay your premiums? *"Yes."* I've been in the business 42 years, and I pay all full premiums every year. There are no bargains. But if at time of sale you say, "All you have to do is pay seven premiums and then don't pay anymore," the guy says "Wow, the other guy said I had to pay to life." He's not a mental midget, so he's going to say, "I'll pay the seven years." Do you pay your premiums? *"Yes."* How long have you been in the business? *"Fourteen years."* What's your income a year? *"Two hundred twenty-five thousand."* You've got a good job. Don't lose the job; there aren't a lot of those out there. But you work hard, too, and you've built a big clientele. You people in this audience are doing very well in our business. But you can do twice what you're doing if you get a little better organized.

Question: A handful of companies have introduced a first-to-die universal life or intrasensitive whole life. What are your feelings on that product?

Savage: I have some of both, because I'm not bright enough to predict the future. Example: If we knew who was going to get elected in November, we wouldn't have to work the rest of our life. Just to digress here a minute: How come, four months before an election, the candidates are 20 points apart? Three months later it's a rat race. How come it never goes to 40 points? I contend: the news media. It becomes a game. They have to work—make things exciting. It's "Here's what this guy said," and they take some little piece out of that, just one little word. But take one little word out of anything . . . you know, years ago I said I voted for one Democratic president, John Kennedy. A guy says, "I know why you voted for him; because he's Catholic." I said, not so; I voted for John Kennedy because *I'm* Catholic. One little change, right?

Question: At the meeting in San Francisco you had a unique idea for your term conversions, when you announced you've got 50 of the good stuff and 450 of the bad stuff. I just thought people would be interested in how you do that.

Of the death claims paid in the United
States for the last 25 straight years,
under 5 percent are for term policies
and 95 percent are for permanent.

Savage: I convert term insurance to permanent when a person is in good shape financially. There's no reason to have term insurance, none. I use a lot of ideas. By the way, I have a philosophy on permanent insurance: If everybody kept it until they died, I don't know if the insurance companies would've made the money they have over the years. What do we know? Insurance companies make more money on the sale of term or permanent? John? *"Term."* Term! Do you know that of the death claims paid in the United States for the last 25 straight years, under 5 percent are for term policies and 95 percent are for permanent? Term policies are actuarily computed not to be enforced when you die. Because the rate keeps going up and up and finally the guy says, "I don't need it anymore." And the insurance company's cheering. "Wow, Charlie was getting close; did he get us off the hook!" But the mental midgets of the world say, "Buy term insurance and invest the difference." Now, what really happens? They buy term insurance and spend the difference. So they end up with insurance and no money. But the beautiful thing about permanent life insurance, and we've seen it time and time again, people needed $60,000, $70,000—it was nice to know they had it for an emergency. Term insurance? A person buys term insurance at age 20, keeps it to age 75. Another buys ordinary life at 20—same amount—and keeps it to 75. What's the difference in premium paid over the whole 55 years? Both people paid exactly the same amount of money. Term insurance is cheaper in the early years, more expensive in the later years—and all ordinary life does is level the premium. But there's a big difference: You get the cash back. Now, you may never use it, and if you die, fine, you don't get it, it's part of the life insurance contract. But it's nice to know it's there if you need it. Term insurance? There's nothing there. The good stuff, you get your money back; the bad stuff, you don't get your money back. Which contract would you like? So, a guy has $50,000 of the good stuff and $450,000 of the bad stuff. It still gives him protection. He asks me:

"John, do you think I'm always going to need $500,000 worth of life insurance?" My answer: No. Why? The way he said that. I mean, you've got to serve the client. The client doesn't want to have $500,000. Then I say, "What do you think?" He says, "John, I think I'm going to be comfortable stopping at a quarter million." I say, "Why don't we stop now? Get a quarter million of permanent, get rid of the rest," and he says, "Boy, that makes sense." That's a good sale. See, the client will dictate, if you're sensitive to the client's needs. And that's what will separate you.

Question: On term or permanent, do you try to convince people that they should have insurance to die with, or, again, do you take your cue from them?

Savage: My job is to serve my clients. I have millions of dollars in term insurance in force on the books. My own is all permanent. I know you can't beat it for estate planning. Term insurance cannot be used for estate planning. It has so much hollow at the top end, I don't know anybody who keeps it very long. Now, you want to talk about an area you haven't touched on; it's interesting.

Let's use a top executive with Ford Motors. He has $2 million in his pension plan; he has $500,000 in his 401(k). He has another million dollars in assets. He and his wife die in a common disaster. Do you have nay idea what the tax is? It's over 80 percent. That's why I get a kick out of people when you ask them, "What are you worth?" Guy says, "I'm worth $2 million." I say, "Well, what is it?" He says, "Well, $1,500,000 is my pension plan; $300,000 is my 401(k)." That has to get taxed three times: income tax, when you take it out; excise tax; and estate tax, for both the state and federal. So his kids are waiting around—three of them—and they've got to figure, "We're worth $2,100,000. We get $700,000 each." They get $33,512 each. So, you should be doing some work with your bigger clients, explaining to them that their estate doesn't really have all the liquidity they think it has. The need for insurance to fill that gap is very, very important.

Question: John, there are short-term needs and long-term needs and then forever needs. Do you select a one-year term for most of your term products?

Savage: I sell one-year term exclusively. I have not sold any other type of term insurance. It's the cheapest and it's short-term. They want the least amount for a short period of time. You can lull them into security if you sell them 10-, 15- or 20-year term.

Question: In High Touch Selling, *you gave an example of where you were teaching a young single man how to save money, and you allowed him to whittle himself down from a suggested $1,000 a month to $500/$400 a month. You took 80 percent of that and put it in the bank and 20 percent in life insurance. What happens if the young man comes back to you and he's goofed up; he hasn't saved the amount of money that you told him to? Instead of having $3,000, he's only saved $1,000; he's taken money out of it. Do you adjust?*

Savage: That happens and happens. The young person comes back and doesn't put the money in he said he would. I have a lot of one-liners: "You can't take care of 23 years of sinning with one year of penance." I say, "Let's see if we can do it this year." I've had people coming in for three or four years and they don't have any money saved. They have the spending disease. I can't change them: I still serve them. I don't spend an extra amount of time with them.

Question: In that interview, you sell the term—I forget how you phrased it exactly—double indemnity (Savage: Automatic double-in-demnity rider), *meaning any time you die we'll pay as if you've been killed. When you convert that in a subsequent year, do you do that by putting less in the bank or by increasing the monthly check-o-matic by the new increased premium?*

Savage: Say you sell $50,000 whole life and you had $50,000 one-year term—you're only about $2.65 a month, or $3.12 a month. Then I say to the client, "Would it make any difference if your premium was $36 dollars or $39.12 a month if we could double your coverage? He says no. See, term insurance is very important when you're young. You've got the family. But boy, oh boy, I have difficulty having it after you're 55 years of age, unless you got married late and had a big family.

Question: How do you know what the premium is if you haven't run a proposal?

Savage: That's an interesting question. How many ages are there that you're going to sell? About 40. Could you go home this weekend and, in the three contracts that you sell, memorize what the premium is at each age? Would you do that? *"Yes "* So simple Thrs rs what you're doing for a *living,* folks. Do you ever watch your secretary type? Doesn't look at A, S, D—doesn't look at em. I go A. . . S. . . D. I don't type. You should know what the premium is at every age. How many contracts do you sell? *"About five or six."* How many do you sell? *"The same." "Two."* Most of your policies are sold from age 20 to 40. Now I've really cut your work down. Every question like that, I say to a person, "Could you double your production if you knew you were going to be shot at the end of the year if you didn't?" He says, "Why, sure!" I say, "You're one bullet away from doubling you production." How can you walk around, you're in this business, and you don't know the rates!? The rates!! That's what it costs! Imagine going into a car dealer's shop, and grabbing a guy who's been there six months: "What does a Buick Riviera cost?" And he says, "Sir, that's $17,250." Price. Cost. Value. We are an amazing group of people. We know everything about everything except what the customer wants to know. What does it cost? Guy says, "Just a second." Gets the book out. Calls the secretary in. Runs a print-out. Fifteen minutes later the guy's cleaning his nails, walking the floor, and you come back and say, "It's $36 a month." And he says, "I must have the dumbest agent in the world."

PART THREE

Clients on Savage

Editor's note: The vast majority of this book consists of observations, opinions and procedures generated by John F. Savage. Their purpose is to provide a guide that professional salespeople can adapt to their individual needs, to better serve their clients and, in the process, forge a more successful, personally satisfying career. However, this portion of the book offers the perspectives of some of John's clients, as told to David M. Drury, who assisted John in the writing of this book. In essence, what follows are the appraisals of very talented, seasoned executives—how they size up the author in terms of what he has provided them over the years.

16

Client Perspectives

Harold A. McMaster, chairman of the board, Glasstech, Inc., Perrysburg, Ohio; 300 employees; glass heat-treating and bending equipment for the architectural and automotive trades. McMaster is personally responsible for approximately 80 of his firm's 100-plus patents; more are pending.

I first met John in the early 1980s, through a colleague and mutual acquaintance. It was just a hello/goodbye kind of encounter. Parenthetically, I should say I'd always been leery of insurance peddlers—you know, the old stereotype of their wanting to make a sale regardless of what you actually could use. Well, it developed that John seemed to have talents aside from insurance that I thought might be useful. I accepted his offer to help in any way he could, short of buying insurance. I soon learned that he could apply an almost infallible "smell test": That is, he can spot a phony in nothing flat; he can look over a field of executive candidates and quickly identify those who are capable of assuming greater responsibilities as opposed to those who are not up to the challenge but who think they are. When I headed up a preceding company, PermaGlass, it had grown to 550 employees and become very complex. If I had had John as an adviser in those days, I probably would have been able to surmount those challenges, instead of cutting loose to form a smaller Glasstech.

I also could have used John's advice before I gave significant gifts to Defiance College and to the University of Toledo. Fortunately, he came on the scene to counsel me prior to my gift to Bowling Green State University. Briefly, he convinced me to use insurance policies as the basis for a present to BGSU, thereby substantially reducing what would otherwise have gone to inheritance taxes.

Similarly, he's pored through literally countless proposals I've received for investment opportunities, winnowed out a batch of dubious pitches and given me strong—and subsequently accurate—recommendations on a dozen or so profitable ones. He has a keen knack for forming sound judgments after assembling sometimes elusive facts.

He's raised tens of millions of dollars in charitable contributions for a variety of causes, primarily educational and religious. Perhaps lesser known is his ability to raise funds for private enterprises such as my own. Back in 1987, we needed $15 million to proceed with our plans for photovoltaic panels. John raised the great majority of that sum in Toledo (Ohio) alone. It's merely an example of how his reputation for trust and integrity has taken hold. Why, I bought into The Andersons on John's say-so alone; I never looked at a word of their descriptive materials.

Along the way, I eventually bought insurance from John, as have so many others of my acquaintance, with my strong endorsement. To John, it's always been a gentlemanly quid pro quo. He offers to help you any way he can. The understanding is that if you benefit from such assistance and are in the market to buy some insurance, you'll buy it from him. That's it—period. I've gotten more out of this arrangement than I ever bargained for. In the process, I've come to know and appreciate a caring man of deep principles—a person who can give great motivational and inspirational speeches not only because he has the ability to communicate to virtually any audience, but also because he knows his convictions to the letter and doesn't hesitate to state them in very emphatic terms to those who care to listen.

Richard P. Anderson, president and chief executive officer of The Andersons; 2,400 employees. Firm has grown since 1947 into a multifaceted enterprise headquartered in Maumee, Ohio, that includes ten grain elevator plants with storage capacity for 50 million bushels, five general stores doing a combined $750 million annually in retail trade and other core businesses (corncob milling, lawn products, absorbents, chemicals and railroad car renovation).

I didn't make any notes to prepare for this interview; what I say is right off the top of my head. John's main characteristics are very unusual, perhaps unique. I've never met anyone else like him. I don't think he's "duplicatable." First off, he's consistently positive—always. I've never known him to be "down," not even when he's suffered and been in life-threatening situations. He simply doesn't *allow* himself to lose control or indulge in self-pity. He always sets his sights on positive *results*, doesn't bother himself with petty details and drives right for the solution or bottom line. Keep it simple! He projects hard-earned, hard-held principles and is unequivocal in laying them out. On the other hand, I've never seen him as arbitrary. He'll listen carefully, make a concession on a detail (never a principle) when it's logically called for, then go on from there. And it's just amazing how that method of operation has a way of keeping a discussion headed in a direction the participants ultimately agree is sound, based on reasonable give and take.

Of course, that appraisal came after I'd already sized John up on his most fundamental results, points that count most with me (and my wife, Fran) as an individual and as husband and parent. In his spiritual realm, John's religion is Number One. On the temporal side, it's Kate and their kids. That family is as complete and attentive to one another as anybody could hope for. It's the dividend for a lifetime of mutual love and hard work. I also know I'm not alone in that evaluation. He's held in high esteem literally worldwide, not only because he can deliver the goods via business ability and a remarkable speaking capacity, but because he comes across as positive-personified: smart, caring, principled. As a listener—and I've heard him speak many times—I used to wonder why I enjoyed his speeches so much. To me, they're like my favorite music. They just make me feel good.

As for specific examples of how he's served The Andersons—and me—over the years, they're virtually beyond count. But here's one recent case: Ours is a family-structured business. We elected years ago to spread that ownership equally to all generations, with a huge generation coming along. Our shares were not traded. As the youngsters matured, married, moved away, invested in other things, built homes and so forth, there was a natural need to trade some shares. So John told me he thought there were a lot of people who'd like to buy those shares. In spite of the fact that our earnings, while not negative, had not been comparable to other investments, John said he still thought people would want to invest in our company, adding that he was positive we could sell what we wanted to sell. So we decided to take a 10 percent piece and see what happened. That came to $5 million. Very quietly, without charging us anything, John went to his clientele and got the $5 million committed over a period of six months. I don't know if anything like that has ever been done before. From the very outset, he assured me there'd be nothing to it—"it's all in the bag." It seemed so overly optimistic. But, typically, he delivered—to the dismay of many of the onlookers. He simply has an awesome talent for raising huge amounts of money, whether it be for charities or private enterprise. Being extraordinarily generous himself, he can and does ask for large contributions. He's solicited me on a number of occasions. I've always known what he was up to, but I could never quite put my finger on just when in the conversation I agreed to contribute to whatever cause he was serving at the time.

Could John have been a success in some other capacity, say as a big corporate CEO, like my position? He could probably succeed at anything he set his mind to. He has such an intelligent, disciplined mind. On the other hand, I know he couldn't be bothered with all the monkey business I have to put up with. Then there's his "untidy" (unorthodox) style. In my own case, and I'm sure it's the same with many others, he just walks in on me anytime the notion hits him. He won't fuss with making an appointment or sticking with a prescribed schedule, or hanging around in a lobby. And when he shows up, I'll just listen to what he has to say, whatever the subject. I know he'll get to the point, won't harp, won't recite a lot of details (because he's not impressed with minutiae he doesn't understand and that are aside from the essentials of people and bottom lines). A genuine original. Colleagues would do well to try to pick up on some of his techniques. But I know I couldn't begin to do what he's done. Like I said, he's beyond duplication.

John C. Bates, president and CEO of privately held Heidtman Steel Products, Inc. (part of Centaur, Inc., a holding company for various steel as well as nonsteel companies—e.g., trucking). Started with Heidtman in 1962 (four employees, $267,000 in annual sales). Assumed leadership in 1983. Currently 1,050 employees in several states; $300 million in annual sales.

Our business has expanded during a 30-year period when the nation's steel industry has been contracting. We've grown at the expense of others who don't invest in their people and plants. We invest constantly and heavily in both, but mostly in people. John Savage has been of exceptional value in helping us in the most critical phase of any business—that is, in motivating our employees, especially our production workers. This doesn't mean he hasn't been advantageous for our executives; he certainly has been. It's just that pumping up the production crew is a much tougher, ongoing challenge. For this, John has the remarkable knack of boosting morale, instilling a real sense of teamwork and making people feel good about themselves and about being successful. To be truly successful, a person can't split his principles. They have to be carried through consistently, across the board. John knows how to get that message straight to the target, and always with humorous touches. People invariably remember more than one of the things he tells them, but the point gets down to how to be a better person and that there is a right way and a wrong way to treat people.

On a personal level, I always look forward to meeting with John one-on-one. We share a mutual commitment to a strong moral base in both human and business relationships. And I always come away from a meeting with him, usually over breakfast, feeling I've gained new or better insights. His advice and every other service, other than the selling of an insurance policy, is free—invaluable and beyond the measure of any price tag.

Once you get to know him, you recognize that John is a genuine "handshake" kind of guy. You can literally bank on his word; more than knowledgeable, completely trustworthy.

Coincidentally, John was a link to what developed into a multimillion-dollar joint venture I struck, on a handshake, with Henry Hillman, of Pittsburgh. Documentation for the partnership was worked out in February 1992. That's the way John and I, and our contacts, operate. Deal with people who have a lot of integrity and in whom you have trust. We don't come armed with a bunch of attorneys to nit-pick. Know who you're dealing with, cut through the tape, avoid time-killing delays, reach an understanding, shake hands on it—and get on with business.

Even so, it's still hard work and long hours; mine average 12 a day. I know John has also been a hard driver throughout his career as both insurance representative and husband and father. And I'm convinced hard work is what our nation has to accept for economic survival. We have perhaps 40 million citizens who are unproductive, many going from one generation to the next on handouts. But we also have 200 million who are the productive side of the ledger—and that's a lot of good worker material. Trouble is, too many are in low-paying service jobs; in our tri-state area of Ohio, Michigan and Indiana, the average for a service industry employee is $11,000 a year. That's not the kind of money that'll buy a car or house; it's just enough to scrape by. On the other hand, the average manufacturing wage in the same area is $31,000. That's purchasing power, the power needed to lift the economy.

John Savage knows far better than most that our society cannot move ahead when our employment growth is tied to people making hamburgers instead of durable products. It's why he's so dedicated to education, to personal improvement—training colleagues, instructing the young, pushing for a college degree in sales (a really great idea!).

Rene McPherson, currently active as a member on six boards and in various family enterprises. Former dean of the Graduate School of Business, Stanford University. Started in 1952 as a sales engineer at Dana Corporation, retiring in 1980 as chairman/CEO. In that interim, sales rose from $155 million to $2½ billion and 27,000 U.S. employees, 80 percent of whom owned stock in the corporation.

I think that the characteristic most accountable for John Savage's success is—and I'm not a Bible-thumper, by any means—his being the most "natural" Christian I've ever met. He is totally at peace in his position with the Lord. This, in turn, has given him an unassailable foundation, where "John is John"—what you see is what you get, no matter how high or low your rank may be. He treats everyone the same. He doesn't suffer fools gladly. He'll simply avoid them, which is their loss. If he were to do something different from his present occupation, I can't think of anything he'd be better at than serving on corporate boards. All told, I've been on 27 of them and am left with the conclusion that 80 percent of board members are worthless; they are the servants of CEOs, who are superb salesmen, rather than being their directors

With John, that kind of role reversal just couldn't happen. He has an absolute genius for casting aside yards of insignificant details, ignoring con games, cutting to the heart of a problem, then prescribing remedies. Through it all, he has that fantastic, positive approach to everything. And that makes him what I call a "Tomorrow" guy—a proactive philosophy that prods you to look down the road and anticipate the inevitable bumps. For example, it's not just who should be next in the line of succession, but who's next after who's next. Most of us don't like to think about successors, or what's of concern beyond today. Not John; he's superb at and will not be diverted from projecting. Many times he's called me and said, "Hey, Rene, we've not talked much about 'tomorrow.'" In doing so, he refocuses all of us on what really matters—ethics. What do we stand for? As a terrific salesman, he can pose those critical questions: Are you selling better? Is the next generation ready? And he does it all with a complete lack of pretension. I've seen it many times: He walks into a meeting and doesn't look, think or act like a big shot. To the uninitiated, he'd probably be sized up as a head statistician or some other functionary. They simply aren't prepared for him. But give him a half hour and it's "gotcha!" That's rare, and I've been blessed in having had the opportunity to see that rarity.

Index